Foreword

Captured by the Bamboozle!

I have a special gift in mind for you, one that I promise will profoundly transform your life and the lives of your loved ones. Imagine the joyous anticipation of knowing that you found a treasure map. The scent of excitement fills the air as you hold that object in your hands, the answer to your financial future. You know where the "X" is. Pass this wealth on and watch as the ripple effect spreads throughout your friends and family.

I went to the theater recently and noticed a sign about movie ratings. The sign said that in order for the rating system to be effective, you need to understand the system. Similarly, understanding how finance works is important. Solving a complex puzzle is like thinking critically instead of mindlessly adhering to generic advice. Carl Segan said, "We simply accepted what the most widely available and accessible source of information claimed is true. For our naiveté we are systematically misled and bamboozled." One of the saddest lessons of history is this: If we've been bamboozled long enough, we tend to reject any evidence of the **bamboozle**. We're no longer interested in finding out the truth. The "Bamboozle" has captured us. The realization is just too agonizing to admit, even to ourselves, that we've been deceived. Once you grant a charlatan authority over you, you almost never regain control. Many times, we cling to common beliefs even when they have been proven false, solely to avoid experiencing embarrassment. The great philosopher Jim Rohn said; "You can stand in your garden and say there's no weeds, there's no weeds but weeds will take your garden." You must take action! Whether we admit it or not, we are all involved in conflict with the financial industry, and we lack the tools for this fight. They have full control over information and manipulate the data to their advantage. I am not merely a "Whistle Blower" but also an arms dealer, ready to equip you with the most formidable weapon ever created by humans, available for free download; the BAII Plus financial calculator by Texas Instruments, it's a window to the truth. Like Wonder Woman's rope it forces anyone held by it to tell and understand the absolute truth. When you learn how to manipulate a BA II no one will be able to financially bamboozle you again. You will hold in your hands all the weapons you need. It's like flipping on the lights in a dark room. You may find that I'm too emotional and use too strong of a language but as you read more I hope my enthusiasm is infectious. I pray this is a vaccine that will change your financial health. When I hear people tell me to, "Tone it down". It's like when women asks my grandmother if she could stop my grandfather from saying; "Manure"? She told her "No!" The process of getting him to say manure took me years. This is me calmed down.

The world would benefit if high schools taught BAII Plus classes. To send our kids out into this world of wolves, unarmed, is unforgiveable.

This book is about a way to prosper in the coming hard times, but to understand this book you must understand how to use this weapon system; BAII Plus Financial Calculator. I've included a training manual at no charge. I know you are anxious to get into this book but since you are reading the Foreword you must be inquisitive and conscientious; you are someone who is not lazy and wishes to do what's right.

You can download BAII Plus for free from your App Store. A BAII Plus and this manual will change your life and give you ultimate power against the "Bamboozle"! Take a moment to read a portion of the book and subsequently challenge yourself with math. I assure you that this will bring a smile to your face, as you'll no longer be deceived by the financial industry. A good friend of mine was just deceived with a PayPal scam. I stated this because of the horrible effect that scam had on her. Loss of money was bad enough but the feeling of being stupid and vulnerable darkened her soul for weeks. Picture the emotions that would arise if the financial industry deceived you and you only discovered it when it was too late in life to rectify the situation. The great philosopher Jim Rohn said: "We must all suffer from one of two pains: the pain of discipline or the pain of regret." Twenty years from now, I hope you don't discover that the pain of discipline is small but the pain of regret is enormous.

*****

Shelter From the Storm

Chapter 1

Killing The Wolves

The movie "Wolf of Wall Street" is about the financial industry, which is engaged in rampant corruption and fraud, leading to client's downfall. The narrative was a captivating work of fiction centered on a man, Jordan Belfort referred to as "The Wolf of Wall Street," however, it is important to note that he was not the only individual involved. The financial industry became infested with many packs of wolves. Those Goliath industries are a breeding ground for moral ambiguity, where victims are met with a cold lack of sympathy. These so-called legitimate industries are stocked with cubs who gnawed their way out of a bitch wolf's womb, put-on three-piece suits and headphones, then went hunting for innocent prey. They are truly "Wolves in Sheep's Clothing," their piercing eyes gleaming with hidden motives, their voices laced with deceitful charm. The air around them carries a sense of unease, as if a foul stench lingers beneath their innocent facade. The truth remained concealed so deeply, that even a cadaver dog would have difficulty in revealing it, yet I happened upon it. When I mustered the courage to expose the truth, they launched an onslaught, determined to bury me in a labyrinth of darkness, erasing any trace of my existence. Their relentless efforts created a suffocating silence, as if the world held its breath, refusing to acknowledge my words. They are reminiscent of the ancient doctors who, convinced of their noble intentions, would compassionately drain the blood of afflicted patients, their actions accompanied by the metallic scent of blood and the anguished cries of the sick. They've concealed their own truths within a multitude of lies, causing me to doubt if even 1% of them remember their true identity as wolves. Wolves scam us repeatedly throughout multiple generations. They learned how to lie to themselves and believe it and what's worse they have learned how to sell all of us those very lies. The fine print lies are so artfully concealed that their creators become deluded, convinced of their own falsehoods amidst a tapestry of deception. A mental health condition known as antisocial personality disorder or sociopathy exists, in which an individual consistently demonstrates a lack of concern for ethical principles, disregarding the rights and emotions of others. In my opinion, this definition covers various areas in the financial industry, spanning from banking to investments. Make no mistake, the wolf species may not all look the same, but deep down they will always aim for your throat. The species are all wolves, but I will break each one down with their bread. The different breads of wolves are banking, life insurance, annuities, mortgages, credit cards, and the IRS. No matter how strong they are or how dangerously they divert from the truth. Everything they do is designed to take your money and make money with it; OPM (Other Peoples' Money).

*****

Chapter 2

Most of Our Limitations Are Self-imposed

It is necessary for me to provide an explanation for why I am undertaking this task. Thirteen years ago, I fearlessly confronted the financial industry, firmly believing in the power of truth to lead me to victory. Unbeknownst to me, my assumptions proved too far from reality. I experienced a sense of vulnerability and exposure, as if I were a piece of meat tossed to ravenous wolves. Their response only awakened a sleeping giant and filled me with a great resolve. If you want to arm yourself with the truth, then read on. If you dedicate some time and embrace an open mind, refrain from judgment, seek the truth, and then decide, I believe you'll concur that my endeavors to educate you were valuable, despite the price I paid.

I'm reminded of the speech Billy Bob Thorton delivered in "Friday Night Lights"; It's about you and your relationship with yourself, your family, and your friends. Being perfect is about being able to look your friends in the eye and know that you didn't let them down because you told them the truth. And that truth is you did everything within your capabilities. It wasn't possible to do anything else. Can you live in that moment as best you can, with clear eyes, with joy in your heart? If you can do that gentleman- you're perfect!" This is my attempt at being "Perfect".

You may have to read this book a few times. My revolutionary ideas are akin to a smooth stone breaking the surface of a serene pond. The tranquil water resists its impact, creating ripples in the air, the sound reverberating like a melodic symphony. The scent of anticipation lingers in the atmosphere as the water, reluctant at first, resists the foreign intrusion. Yet, with persistence, my ideas permeate the depths of the pond, finally embraced in a moment of complete acceptance. Or you may doubt what I say but I paid a very heavy price to say it. If what I say is not accepted I don't feel bad because I did all I could do, and all I can do is all I can do.

*****

Chapter 3

Werewolves

Werewolf movies have become increasingly popular in recent times, captivating audiences with their thrilling visuals, bone-chilling sounds, and intense atmosphere. Their plots both captivate and mesmerize us as they often revolve around a gentle, pure-hearted individual who, through no fault of their own, is ruthlessly attacked by a malevolent creature that forever craves the essence of human blood. The scene unfolds with a chilling ambiance, as the sharp sound of the monster's fangs piercing the innocent victim's flesh echoes through the air. The scent of blood lingers, mingling with the fear-induced sweat that permeates the atmosphere. In this haunting moment, a sense of dread and fascination intertwine, enveloping us in the enigmatic world of these dark and tragic tales. The monstrous creature, with its feral eyes glinting in the darkness, is unable to restrain its insatiable desire to feast upon humanity, for its survival hinges on the crimson life force that courses through our veins. The pungent scent of desperation and fear permeates the air as the beast's ravenous hunger grows, its existence teetering on the precipice of annihilation. It does what it must do to survive and even though we may despise it, we also must, at some basic level of our humanity, understand its motivation to survive. When our very existence is at stake, the deafening roar of urgency fills the air, igniting a fire within us. Our vision sharpens, focusing on the task at hand, as the scent of determination lingers in the atmosphere. Every fiber of our being trembles with an unparalleled sense of purpose, propelling us forward. It's an inborn desire to survive.

I once came across an intriguing article mentioning that cats produce a hormone in their excrement. This hormone, when consumed by mice, somehow diminishes their innate fear of cats, making them vulnerable and easy targets. That is exactly what has happened to us. We didn't consume their wolf feces, but we fully embraced their deceptive narrative. The stench of their lies permeated the air, while our senses were overwhelmed by the sights and sounds of their manipulative tactics. We unknowingly immersed ourselves in their web of deceit, feeling the weight of their falsehoods burden our trust. With the primal instinct to survive pulsating within you, I invite you to witness the elaborate dance that coerced you into relinquishing your innate commonsense. Picture a scene where the cacophony of persuasive voices echoes in your ears, their words weaving a web of deception. The air is heavy with the scent of manipulation, as your senses are overwhelmed by a relentless onslaught of clever tactics. In this disorienting haze, the world swirls around you, blurring your vision and distorting reality. The cacophony of dissonant sounds overwhelms your ears, disorienting you further. A pungent smell hangs in the air, adding to the sense of unease. As reason slips away from your grasp, your mind becomes vulnerable prey to their cunning schemes. This ability is not exclusive to the educated; it is a universal susceptibility. You lose your ability to make decisions based on logic and reason. They use every one of our senses to manipulate us into their fangs. There's a vast gulf stretching before us, like an endless expanse of untouched land, separating commonsense from conventional wisdom. Commonsense, like the vibrant hues of a sunset painting the sky, stems from our personal observations, while conventional wisdom, like a symphony of voices harmonizing in the air, represents an accumulation of other people's thoughts. We are often deceived when we have doubts about ourselves, and someone exploits that to make us abandon our knowledge and conform to the popular opinion. Like the fairy tale, “The Emperor’s New Clothes. An emperor engages the services of two tailors who guarantee to create a truly remarkable ensemble for him. These clothes, they claim, will possess the extraordinary quality of being completely invisible to anyone who lacks competence or intelligence. When the emperor goes to see his new clothes, he sees nothing at all — for the tailors are swindlers and there aren't any clothes. Blinded by darkness, he kneads his own intelligence, desperately pretending to catch a glimpse of their elusive presence. The silent whispers of doubt fill the air, mingling with the scent of uncertainty. An invisible weight presses upon him, urging him to avoid the humiliation of looking foolish. The Emperor's New Clothes is an allegory for economic injustice: It proposes that the weavers from the bedtime story are analogous to today's bankers, bond dealers, traders, insurance companies, and hedge-fund managers. However, in the midst of the hushed whispers and gasps, a young child's voice pierces the air, exclaiming with innocent boldness that the emperor stands bare before them. The words reverberate, creating a wave of shock and realization that shatters the illusion of the emperor's new clothes. The collective gasp is followed by a symphony of voices, rising in a cacophony of truth, as the once seemingly opulent garments dissolve into the cold reality of the nakedness beneath. But the emperor chooses to ignore the townspeople and continue his procession. For the child's shout that the

“Emperor Wears No Clothes” at the end of the story transforms the tale into a satire with even more of a bite: it reveals how easily people can take up a pretense, but also, conversely, how easily they can be snapped out of such nonsense. It is all about the psychology of the "mob" or the majority. No one desires to be the solitary voice crying out in the wilderness, bursting the bubble. So far, no one has paid me any attention. I am that determined child, trying to awaken you from their bewildering financial labyrinth. With relentless determination, I will delicately peel back the layers of skin, unveiling the concealed reality beneath, exposing "The Naked Truth". You need to be able to tell the good guys from the bad, so as we go through these stories I will give you some background information. You will not be able to accept the naked truth; you are like a kite; you need the wind and a tail and what's most important you need a restraining string to understand how and why the system works. The first thing you need to understand is that the Baby Boomers are driving this economy, but they are victims of the current situation, similar to everyone else.

The only thing remarkable about a Baby Boomer is that every day that one of them was born, so were 9,999 others, and this continued for 18 years, from 1946 to 1964. They have a great effect on any market they enter. Their parents experienced World War II, a battle filled with the deafening roar of gunfire, the acrid smell of smoke and burning debris, and the chilling sensation of fear mixed with determination. They bravely stood against evil, triumphing in the face of unimaginable adversity. They made the world a better, brighter place. Baby Boomers were nurtured by a special generation who displayed the courage to confront a formidable enemy, seizing the enemy by the neck and vigorously shaking the enemy until the enemy surrendered and collapsed to its knees. While the impact of their bravery on world history is undoubtedly significant, the influence that Baby Boomers will exert on the world is poised to be even more substantial. The events I will predict in this book were not part of the plans of the Baby Boomer Generation. They were devoid of any malevolent intentions, but the consequences of their actions stemmed from their ignorance, arrogance, and sheer foolishness. All of us were fooled by what we refer to as "conventional wisdom". “Wolf shit”. The experts exude an air of competence, with their crisp attire and polished appearance. Their confident strides echo through the room, as they carry themselves with an air of authority. As they engage in deep discussions, their voices resonate with wisdom. Merely through observation, we can't help but feel reassured, as they embody the image of what we all envision an expert to be. With their confident demeanor and impeccable attire and all those letters after their names, they effortlessly deceived us, their words dripping with authority. The room buzzed with the sound of their persuasive arguments, a symphony of convincing tones. We couldn't help but experience a blend of awe and vulnerability in their presence, as they skillfully manipulated our trust. A master chess player plans many moves in advance, but these so-called experts manipulated the chess pieces of our lives with no consideration for us, we are the pawns. They are a mercenary group whose only motive is quick profit.

Now I'm not saying that they are evil, but only fools. My definition of a fool is someone who lies to themselves and believes. An industry that is foolish does not have to be a proficient deceiver if they sincerely think their own lie is the truth. After all, if they are salespeople they only must lie to one person: themselves. Once they believe in their lie, they can be very sincere, but they might be sincerely wrong. I've been guilty of that human, erroneous thought process myself. During the housing boom, I had the impression that the value of houses could continue to rise. The "Housing Bubble" is almost insignificant when compared with the soon to arrive "Perfect Storm”.

The charismatic politicians mesmerized us with their persuasive words, painting a vivid picture of the Social Security system that provided a safety net for older adults. They assured us that retirement would perpetually be rejuvenated by the next generation, filling the air with hope and optimism for the future. In this book, I will meticulously dissect this fallacy, unraveling its flawed conclusion like a skilled surgeon meticulously peeling back layers of tissue. I will guide you through the intricate maze of faulty reasoning, shedding light on its concealed flaws. With each turn of the page, you will hear the resolute crack of fallacy crumbling under the weight of logical scrutiny. Together, we will unravel this fallacy, revealing the truth that lies hidden beneath its deceptive facade. In my opinion, as the older 1/3 of the Baby Boomers approach retirement age, the system will start to collapse. The only thing that will keep it alive will be the blood of the Millennials. The survival of the Baby Boomers as they age will determine their reliance on the younger generation for financial support. Being retired and unable to earn money, they still require funds to sustain themselves. Unfortunately, similar to the werewolves mentioned earlier, they have limited options, especially since the renowned suicide doctor, Dr. Kevorkian, has passed away. They will be forced to suck the blood of younger generations or die. I'm saying this so you understand; the Baby Boomers didn't plan this so don't hate them for the situation they find themselves in. We need to look a few moves ahead. I will break down the cause effect of many poor decisions that set up the oncoming disaster. But before I get into the terrible truths and depress you beyond repair, I will show you how to fix your future, how to kill the "Wolves". Normally, I would state the problem and provide the solution, but I'm going to switch things around. I'm going to state the solution so you can read about the problem without fear, knowing a way out and a bright side of the road exist. Like the 'Greatest Generation we all must be brave enough to stand up in front of an evil giant, grab it by the neck and shake it until it gives up and falls to its knees. To do that, you will need to arm yourself with a powerful weapon, the commonsense truth, and an action plan. Reset your mind and be open to shedding old paradigms to achieve this.

One of the most notable features of living in Albuquerque, New Mexico, was the chance to ride my dirt bike in the expansive desert on the western outskirts of the city. One sunny day, as I ventured near the Puerco River, I found myself riding alongside a desolate dry gorge. The tranquility of the surroundings was shattered solely by the thumping of my engine. The scent of dry earth and distant wildflowers filled the air, mingling with the warmth of the sun on my skin. Amidst this tranquil setting, something peculiar caught my attention, captivating my gaze. As I looked down into the depths of the gorge, I found myself shocked by the sight of what seemed to be a desiccated carcass of a cow. The air carried a heavy stench of decay. However, to my astonishment, the seemingly lifeless creature stirred as the sound of my engine reached its ears. I came to a halt, captivated by the sight of the cow. I stood there for a moment, observing its plight. The parched creature seemed to struggle for water, its cracked lips and sunken eyes mirroring its sheer desperation. The scorching heat radiated off its body, intensifying the atmosphere. The parched air bore the unmistakable aroma death as a dozen vultures lazily circling above in their patient dance for lunch, intensifying the cow's desperate thirst. In the midst of this torment, I recognized a river not over 150 yards away, with its waters shimmering. The only available exit from the gorge was at the river. A short while ago, I had been happily frolicking in the crystal-clear water, its brilliance shining under the radiant sun. The gentle lapping of the waves against the shore filled my ears, creating a soothing melody. The invigorating scent of the water permeated the air, refreshing my senses. As I touched the wet sand with my fingertips, I was able to sense the cool moisture lingering, confirming that it had not yet dried. I rode down into the gorge and tried to shoo the cow to the water, but as we got closer, the gorge narrowed to about 4 feet wide. The wind blew 5 or 6 tumble weeds into the narrow part, causing them to become stuck and block passage. Evidently, the cow displayed uncertainty about her capability to push 5 or 6, 10 oz tumble weeds. She charged in the wrong direction, as if I contributed to her troubles. I know she did not act like a bull, but when a 300-pound cow charges, you become a Bull Fighter and step aside, ole. Next, I went down to the tumbleweeds and cleared them from the path, subsequently making my way back to my unintelligent friend. I returned her to the same spot where she previously charged me and she stopped again, but this time there were no tumble weeds present. She looked at me with her heavy-lidded, sorrowful eyes, resembling those of a weary cow. In her thoughts, she acknowledged that the passage was obstructed. Her large, watery eyes remained fixed on me, refusing to budge. Shouting and waving my arms didn't budge her. I searched my surroundings for a stick or something to poke her with, but all I discovered was a dirt clod. I took that dirt cloud and with a light throw hit her right between those big brown sad and stubborn eyes. She wheeled around and took off running in an uneven gate to the river, forgetting all about those old tumble weeds by the time I returned to my bike, she stood ankle deep in the river, emitting a loud sucking sound.

In my opinion, sometimes we conduct ourselves similarly to that cow. We let 5 or 6 conventional wisdom tumble weeds stop us from using our common sense. I promise I won't hit you between the eyes with a dirt clod unless I must. Don't make me hit you between the eyes with a dirt clod. Study the things I am about to teach you and test them for yourself. Run them through your commonsense filter and see if they make sense. Afterward, make a choice and take action.

*****

Chapter 4

Four Primary Tools for Making Money

Now, let's explore the three primary methods through which individuals generate income.

1. Job: It's when your boss discovers a way to capitalize on your skills beyond what he actually compensates you. If something happens to you and you can't work, you don't get paid. You're sacrificing your time to earn money and the amount of time available to you is limited.
2. Small business owner: You now own a job if something happens you don't make any money.
3. Large business owner: If something happens to you and you can't go to work you still get paid but owning an extensive business takes a lot of money.
4. Investor: You don't need to be at work because you used your money to make money, 24 hours a day 7 days a week.

Investing is the best approach, but the challenge lies in finding the funds for investment and deciding on the investment destination. As we move through this book I will teach you where to find the money but first let's look at the four different ways investments make money.

1. Appreciation; The increase in monetary value of real estate and gold. Buy real estate at a cheap price and sell for a higher amount of money. The problem with that situation is that there is always uncertainty involved. I recently came across an intriguing article detailing the

extravagant purchases of renowned individuals, acquiring opulent mansions worth millions of dollars. However, their fortunes take a staggering turn when attempting to sell these palatial estates, losing a substantial two-thirds of their initial investment.

2. Compound interest refers to the interest that is calculated based on both the **principal amount** and the interest that has been accumulated from the previous period. The concept varies from simple interest. Example: You put $1,000 in a savings account at 2%. You will have $1,011.67 at the end of the month. You made $11.67. The next month you will earn $11.68 because your interest is now making more interest.

3. Amortization; This is the process of repayment of debt through periodic installments over a period of time. First let me explain where the word mortgage comes from. It's a compilation of the Latin mort, mortality, death, and the German word, gage; measured. So, mortgage is the measured death of a debt. Einstein stated that compound interest held the highest level of power in the universe, but I regretfully must express a different opinion. It is likely that Einstein did not possess knowledge of amortization. It is possible that he missed it because compound interest is a natural

occurrence and amortization is entirely man made. You know, a couple gets married and brings two kids into the world who quickly enter matrimony and have two children of their own, who then have four children, and so on. According to Robert Kiyosaki, the author of "Rich Dad Poor Dad," the classification of debt is limited to two categories: good debt and bad debt. Good debt is debt that you use to make money like money you borrow to buy income property. Bad debt is debt on a ski boat. But like Einstein he too is wrong. Good debt occurs when someone owes you money and you possess collateral, while bad debt happens when you owe them and they have control over your collateral. Debt is a big moneymaker if you're the lender.

As I reflect on the past, I vividly recall the moment when I finally unraveled the mysteries of the big three. The realization came crashing down on me like a torrential downpour, drenching me with newfound understanding. The sight of my misconceptions crumbling before my eyes both startled and liberated me. The sound of my perspective shattering reverberated through my mind, creating a symphony of clarity. The weight of ignorance lifted from my shoulders, replaced by the exhilarating sensation of knowledge expanding my horizons. A revelation dawned upon me, a void I had been unaware of until the exact moment I hit my forehead with my hand. There was always a missing piece lingering somewhere in the shadows, resembling a faint murmur in the breeze that eluded my grasp. It felt like I stood in a dense forest, encircled by towering trees, yet unable to truly perceive their magnificence until I stepped back. My conclusions all proved to be correct to the extent they reached, but now I recognize I wasn't even in the correct vicinity. My logic was sound, but like Eisenstein said when ask why his final exam had the same questions on it every year; his response was; “The question haven’t changed, but the answers have.”

Before I spill the beans, I want to show what I once thought. Understand I did not make a mistake, my math was accurate, but I failed to see the big picture.

The financial industry is a labyrinth, a maze of misdirection. I only scratched the surface in fifteen years of study. Then, similar to that stone that fiercely skipped along the top of the water, I eventually settled into the dark truth.

*****

Chapter 5

The King of the Money Makers; Amortization

No one has ever said that amortization is the key to wealth before. However, I'm sure you will agree after reading this. Amortization is an accounting technique used to periodically lower the principal of a loan over a set period of time. A loan, amortization, focuses on spreading out loan payments over time so people can afford better houses but the problem is it hides the actual cost. The answerer is easily deciphered with simple math, but "They" confuse it with their mockery of logic.

When the industry wants to sell you on their amortized loan they only inform you about the features that make it look good, which includes a level payment term of the mortgage, helping individuals budget their cash flows over the long term. Like a proficient magician, they effortlessly distract your attention. With a flick of their hand, they make you gaze in one direction, while smoothly shifting the puzzle pieces somewhere else. Realize that what you're hearing is nothing but a concoction of blatant falsehoods, completely untouched and untainted by any trace of truth, BS! Amortized loans are considered beneficial because they always include a principal component in each payment. This indicates that the remaining loan gradually decreases over time. They avoid providing a lengthy explanation about the small portion of your payments allocated towards loan repayment. After you've paid half of the payments you still owe 75% of the principal. The first half is where most of the interest is charged. The reason behind their actions is their awareness of the fact that the average American sells or refinances their house every 5 to 7 years, resulting in most people consistently paying primary interest. When you sell or refinance you lose all the interest you paid and like in Alice in Wonderland you take two steps back for every step forward.

Let me show you how they portray an amortized loan to make it sound positive, but keep in mind that everyone is doing it nowadays, 99% of mortgages are amortized. I will make this simple. You buy a house and finance $100,000 for 30 years at 6%. Your payments are $600. You will witness me talking about what I label as; "Wallet Math". Wallet Math has no connection to the contract you sign but precisely represents the amount of money you truly pay. For example, you borrowed $100,000 and paid back 360 X $600. You paid back $216,000, which amounts to 116% interest instead of 6%.

This is the straightforward math I mentioned earlier.

Allow me to analyze and explain it; So, for every $1 you pay in principal you pay $5 in interest. It is unnecessary to possess exceptional mathematical skills to deduce that it is not 6%. The only real 6% payment you make is the 360th the other 359 are higher. This is the only Truth in Lending there is.

The major disadvantage of amortized loans for borrowers is the small amount of principal paid off in the early stages of the loan, as most of each payment is allocated to interest. Being the lender is the good thing about amortization. This implies that, at the start, there is a limited amount of equity being established for a mortgage. If you sell or refinance the house like most people do within the first 5 to 7 years, you will be surprised at the minimal amount you have paid off. If you possess a mortgage, I recommend examining the amortization table. You will witness it firsthand. If you're a math wise here's the formula:

$$A = P\frac{i(1+i)^n}{(1+i)^n - 1}$$

I cannot comprehend that either. If you lack a mortgage, you can Google Amortization

Schedule and input your own numbers to verify if I'm telling the truth. The Rule of 50/75; after you have paid 50% of the payments you still owe about 75% of the debt. Here's a 30-year amortization table.

Regular Mortgage

first month	Interest	Principal	Balance	Cost I-P
	500.00	99.55	99,900.45	$5.02

Yr. #	Cumulative Interest	Cumulative Principal	Ending Balance	Cost Int. to Prin.
1	5,966.59	1,228.01	98,771.99	$4.86
2	11,857.45	2,531.76	97,468.24	$4.68
3	17,667.89	3,915.93	96,084.07	$4.51
4	23,392.96	5,385.47	94,614.53	$4.34
5	29,027.39	6,945.64	93,054.36	$4.18
6	34,565.59	8,602.05	91,397.95	$4.02
7	40,001.63	10,360.61	89,639.39	$3.86
8	45,329.20	12,227.65	87,772.35	$3.71
9	50,541.62	14,209.83	85,790.17	$3.56
10	55,631.79	16,314.28	83,685.72	$3.41
11	60,592.15	18,548.52	81,451.48	$3.27
12	65,414.72	20,920.56	79,079.44	$3.13
13	70,090.98	23,438.91	76,561.09	$2.99
14	74,611.91	26,112.58	73,887.42	$2.86
15	78,967.94	28,951.16	71,048.84	$2.73
16	83,148.89	31,964.81	68,035.19	$2.60
17	87,143.96	35,164.34	64,835.66	$2.48
18	90,941.70	38,561.21	61,438.79	$2.36
19	94,529.92	42,167.60	57,832.40	$2.24
20	97,895.71	45,996.41	54,003.59	$2.13
21	101,025.35	50,061.38	49,938.62	$2.02
22	103,904.27	54,377.07	45,622.93	$1.91
23	106,517.00	58,958.94	41,041.06	$1.81
24	108,847.14	63,823.41	36,176.59	$1.71
25	110,877.24	68,987.91	31,012.09	$1.61
26	112,588.82	74,470.95	25,529.05	$1.51
27	113,962.21	80,292.16	19,707.84	$1.42
28	114,976.55	86,472.42	13,527.58	$1.33
29	115,609.72	93,033.86	6,966.14	$1.24
30	115,838.19	100,000.00	0.00	$1.16
	115,838.19	**100,000**	**TOTALS**	

Here's an amortization loan for $100,000 at 6% for 30

It shows that after a span of five years, the borrower paid $36,002 and only managed to decrease their principal by $6,945. Now, it's not such a favorable agreement if you are the borrower, but if you were a lender, then it's an extremely profitable deal. If you acted as the bank, you would possess collateral to ensure you wouldn't experience financial loss.

You already know how to lose money with an amortized loan so I'm going to teach you how to use this amazing formula to make money, like a bank.

Understanding amortization isn't as difficult as it may seem once you grasp the purpose of this concept. It did not occur until around 1930 that industry devised this scheme. Certainly, the payment plan was extended to make homeownership more affordable, but that wasn't the primary motivation. The institution took action to boost their own profit, period. The ploy proved too clever, meticulously designed to deceive your senses, and create the illusion of a favor. I have observed this tactic employed in different fields, and this prompts a psychological response that compels you to justify your own actions. I observed the price of gas today and noted that it was $3.45 per gallon. Now, this is a lie I told myself because the gas price wasn't $3.45, but rather $3.45 and 9/10. We deceive ourselves and trust in the falsehood. I need to come to a stop here. Now, before you form an opinion on lenders, you need to understand the legality and public acceptance of their actions. What you should be pondering is, **"How can I gain the knowledge to capitalize on this opportunity and generate wealth akin to a bank? Every loan will appear in this manner, so you must choose whether you want to earn all that money or simply allow the banks to do so, as one of you will.**

There's an old rock and roll song by Dr. John; "Such a Night" that says, "If I don't do it, then somebody else will." If you don't make that profit somebody else will. And that somebody else has always been the banks.

Loan amortization

When you take out a loan, you spread out the cost of the loan over the term of the loan, plus interest. This implies that every month, a portion of the principal (the borrowed amount) along with interest is paid by you. The amount of interest you pay depends on the interest rate on your loan and the term.

Observe the example earlier, where a borrower gets a $100,000 loan at 6% interest for 30 years, resulting in a monthly payment of $600. Out of this amount, $100 represents the principal and $500 represents the interest. Over the course of the loan, the borrower will pay a total of $116,000, in interest and $100,000 in principal. Simply multiply 360 payments X $600 = $216,000. The situation sounds negative, but I want you to approach it from the bank's perspective. In five years, the borrower paid you $36,000, with $29,000 being interest. (I rounded these numbers out to simplify the explanation). For this reason, during Christmas time, banks put up massive Christmas trees, and the borrower has tiny ones. It is a significant profit with minimal risk.

Now when you inquire an expert about what I recently mentioned they will act as if they have known it all along. Everybody in the business wants to give the impression that they comprehend mortgages but if you ask them to explain the concept, you will hear crickets.

Amortization helps make big purchases more affordable, which is beneficial for the economy.

You can spread out the cost of something over time. This implies that you do not need to make the full payment upfront. Without the process of amortization, a housing boom would cease to exist. However, positive aspects should be considered. In reality, the situation is quite the opposite. The scene is filled with activity as I take in the multitude of people engaged in this practice. The air is filled with the sounds of construction and conversations, creating a vibrant atmosphere. That everyone is taking part in this phenomenon is clear, contributing to its widespread nature. So, amortization is a good thing if you are the lender or the US economy but if you are the borrower then that's another story. I don't want to make you angry by showing you how houses are financed. Instead, I want to show you how you can make money like banks do. If you had the ability to utilize the same methods banks use, your perspective on amortization would likely be more favorable.

After I break down the other types of profit-making strategies I will explain how you can make money like a bank.

Chapter 6

Real Estate

I don't want to give the wrong impression, but let me tell you, real estate has a way of captivating the senses. The sight of luxurious properties and bustling open houses, the sound of negotiations and construction echoing through the air, the smell of fresh paint and new beginnings. And let's not overlook the exhilarating and hopeful sensation that accompanies observing individuals generate wealth in the realm of real estate. When you own real estate you want everyone to know. While the world of real estate may dazzle with its captivating allure, its efficiency often falls short. The bustling streets lined with towering buildings, the symphony of honking horns and bustling footsteps, and the palpable energy in the air - all contribute to the excitement and hypnotic nature of this industry. However, underneath the surface exists a reality that is far from efficient. Nevertheless, when it comes to genres, banks tend to generate higher profits from real estate due to their ability to profit from both buying and selling properties. The banks earn money from both sellers and owners in every transaction requiring financing. After paying what I call Amtax ("The Amortization Tax") all profits are diminished substantially. I'll explain Amtax later.

Real Estate, similar to gold, doesn't benefit from all 3 ways of making money. My wise old dad once told me in life, victory doesn't always favor the strongest, nor does success always belong to the quickest, but those are the ones you should bet on. I compare real estate and gold to boxing; both of them might finish the fight but neither one is a winner; they both just got some good punches in. I like to bet on something that maximizes profit while minimizing risk but I found that people seem to ignore the thing that does that. If real estate is your passion, then you have my full support, and this book contains valuable insights on how to generate income. But remember, you can drive a nail with a rock, but a hammer is a lot easier.

Most profits in real estate are generated when you acquire the property, rather than when you sell or get rid of the property. If you buy an asset at a low cost and its value rises, selling can result in a substantial profit. I've witnessed real estate fluctuate in both directions many times, so if you purchase when the market is at its peak and circumstances force you to sell when the market is at its lowest, there is only devaluation, and you have no authority over the situation. Timing is your enemy; too many people leave time out of their financial decisions. Frank Sinatra sang; "Luck Be a Lady Tonight" and most of the time; "timing is just pure luck. In the real estate and stock market industries, fluctuations are always present. You're like a hot air balloon; you go where the wind blows you. So, you can only hope for its appreciation. However, countless possibilities can occur. Nobody expects real estate to decrease in value when they make a purchase, but unfortunately, the value often goes down. Look at all the people who are trapped with office space in San Francisco. In either situation, one person wins, and the other person loses. The great humorist Jack Handey, writer of Deep Thought said; "It's easy to sit there and say you'd like to have more money. And I guess that's what I like about it. It's easy. Just sitting there, rocking back and forth, wanting for that money."

Once more, the equity growth in real estate simply remains there on the porch rocking back and forth, going nowhere. The true impact of the situation becomes clear when you are in the process of paying taxes on or selling the item. You never realize the future value of all your expenses. You can't put equity to work for you even if it's in income property. I'll go into rental property later. You can't make money from compound interest or amortization with real estate; in fact, if you borrow money to purchase real estate, the bankers will use amortization to make more profit than you. A significant amount of money is required to engage in real estate transactions, and you are also constrained by geographical factors and your level of expertise. Most people borrow money to buy real estate and I will show the fallacy of that strategy when I talk about loans. When you borrow money to buy real estate, you're tying a steak around your neck and then trying to run through a wolf infested prairie. There is a plethora of wolf packs that will constantly nip at your heels. Can you make money? Sure; there are always swift deer that outrun the wolves. But you don't see many skinny wolves.

*****

Chapter 7

Gold Is Just Glider

Real estate and gold are two major investments where appreciation is the major profit builder for investors. Appreciation is when you purchase an item and it increases in value, making it the slowest form of investment. During the time you wait for the property to increase in value, there are many expenses that diminish your profit. While the equity remains stagnant, rocking back and forth, it isn't compounding. In fact, it's just sleeping. Appreciation, however, is a two-sided coin. Each winner is accompanied by a loser. The opposite of appreciation is depreciation. Two major forms of appreciation exist. Real estate and gold. You purchase both and have the expectation that their value will increase. It's hard to compare the returns; ROI (Return on Investment) in real estate because there are so many expenses such as inflation, taxes, maintenance, management, insurance, and interest on loans (Amortized Debt). All of these are working against you 24 hours a day 7 days a week. Real estate reminds me of a monkey trapped because he desires the apple in the jar but cannot extract his hand from the bottle's narrow neck while holding it.

I know that owning property is a natural inclination for humans, this concept is widely accepted knowledge. But you're not seeing the big picture which I will show you later.

Let's start by examining the allure of gold. The captivating allure of the shimmering metal showcased in TV ads has always fascinated me.

The vibrant visuals, accompanied by the melodic jingle, ignite a sense of excitement. The faint scent of possibility lingers in the air, as I am drawn to the glossy portrayal of this precious metal. They inform us about the lack of value in our money and how the growing national debt will ultimately render our currency worthless due to inflation. The only way to safeguard our wealth is by purchasing their precious gold. Yet they want us to send them our "worthless money" and they will send us their "precious gold". Why would they desire our "Worthless Money" and why would they be open to exchanging our currency for their "Precious Gold"? While the general belief is that purchasing gold is a smart choice, personally, I find this to be quite unwise, as my own logic suggests. Gold was approximately $1,400 an ounce 5 years ago and despite the national debt more than doubling, gold is currently valued at about $1,900 an ounce. Gold does not have the ability to compound. In order for gold to appreciate money needs to suffer from inflation. In 2021, gold was worth $2,021 an ounce. The value of it dropped to $1,900 today despite inflation reaching a record high. If an object recognizes its worth, it remains idle and dormant unless you trade it. No magical mathematics influences it like compound interest or amortization. The situation is like a rancher who purchases 100 cows and lets them graze in his pasture, consuming his grass and water, but includes no bulls among them. His sole hope of earning money is for all of them to survive, grow fat, and the market to remain stable. Now I'm an amateur on the Bible, but here is what the Bible warns about the evils of holding gold Matthew 25:14-30. The story of a master who left gold with three of his servants. Two put the gold to work and increased its value to which the master rewarded them. (They used it like it was money). The 3rd buried the gold hoping for appreciation before giving it back to the master.

Afterward, the man who had received one bag of gold came. 'Master,' he said, 'I knew that you are a hard man, harvesting where you have not sown and gathering where you have not scattered seed (Using gold like it was money). So, I was afraid and went out and hid your gold in the ground. See, here is what belongs to you.'

"His master replied, 'You wicked, lazy servant! So, you knew that I harvest where I have not sown and gather where I have not scattered seed? Well then, you should have put my money on deposit with the bankers, so that when I returned I would have received it back with interest.

The master said, "Throw that worthless servant outside, into the darkness, where there will be weeping and gnashing of teeth."

I have a friend who told me about the conventional wisdom of buying gold in 2010. He is now gnashing his teeth.

Owning gold is like owning sterile cows; there is no way to produce more cows.

According to the experts, in the event of an economic collapse, gold is the only safe asset to possess. Well bull! The reason gold held value in the first place was due to its rarity, and its ease of being cut up. If a cow had a value of 1/2 ounce of gold, dividing the 1 ounce of gold in half became a simple task. Today, gold is mainly used for jewelry. So, in the event of an economic collapse, would you prefer to possess a piece of jewelry or a rifle for hunting? I have a friend that instead of buying gold buys thousands of rounds of bullets. Gold cannot be ingested, nor can it be employed for shelter. The only purpose for gold in a collapsed economy would be to fashion the metal into bullets so one could hunt game. I suppose you could say, "What knowledge does Mathew possess that eludes those who advocate for gold, specifically in finance?"

*****

Chapter 8

Compound Interest

This book aims to demonstrate the possibility of investing with only a small amount of money and in a safer and more profitable manner. When I first learned about compound interest, I was taught Einstein's Rule of 72. If your savings account is earning 3%, you divide 3 into 72, resulting in 24 years. So, in 24 years, your $2,000 investment would have doubled to $4,000. In 48 years, your total amount will be $8,000, $2,000 of which was originally yours. If a 12% return was being earned, the amount amassed in 48 years would be $512,000. However, it is important to note that banks typically offer a lower interest rate of 3% on savings. However, worth considering is that banks provide a guarantee for your money and the gains it generates. Now you may believe that they don't charge you for that guarantee, but you would be mistaken. If they invested your money by lending it out in credit cards and made 12%, then in 48 years, they would have $512,000 and would pay you the $8,000 that was promised. They made $504,000 using your money. Let me do the math for you. The amount of $875 per month for 48 years is what they charged you for using your money. As I came to this realization, the sight of bustling investors filled the room, the sound of ringing phones echoed in my ears. The scent of freshly printed financial reports wafted through the air, adding to the excitement. I was unable to resist the surge of exhilaration as I sold mutual funds, aware that they were generating an average of 12% per year. Even though the bank's compound interest is safe, the returns sure aren't profitable. If inflation averages 3%, you only reach the breakeven point. I'm unsure of the remaining number of 48-year periods you have, but the availability is likely to be quite limited. I recognized the fact that investing in mutual funds past performance is no assurance of future performance, but the risk appeared worthwhile to me, at the time. I didn’t know anyway for you to make 12% with little risk. Subsequently, I witnessed the stock market experience many booms and crashes. If you required your money during its peak, that was acceptable but if you required it during its decline, you were in significant trouble. If you study the stock market, you realize that it always goes up and down.

For some unexplainable reason, while I was walking my border collie; Cowboys swap their time for money. When they run out of time, they run out of money. Ranchers, however, use compound cattle to make money. In other words, they get their cattle to produce more cattle. They put bulls in the pastures to impregnate the cows and thus the cows produce more cows. Cowboys dream of honkytonks, pickup trucks, and women. Ranchers, however, dream of rain and Horny Cows. You should follow their lead and become money ranchers, Yippee-ki-ay… Gold can't produce more gold, real estate can't produce more real estate but amortization produces more money.

I once lived in the little West Texas town of Ft. Stockton. An old rancher friend of mine, Bulum, told me the story of his ex-best friend Carl and how they became enemies over a misunderstanding of how compound interest works. Carl, filled with wanderlust, longed to embark on an exhilarating voyage, traversing the vast expanse of the world's oceans. Eager to set sail, he approached Bulum, hoping to secure his assistance in taking care of his beloved cattle during his absence. He planned on being gone for a year. Bulum expressed his willingness to help him on the condition of being allowed to graze his cows on Carl's property. Bulum already possessed over a thousand head and 100 more wouldn't make much of a difference to him, so

Carl ensured all his cows were branded, handed Bulum the keys to all his gates, and left 100 head of cattle under Bulum's care. Bulum assured Carl of his intention to return all his branded cows upon his return. One year later, Bulum fulfilled his promise and returned all 100 cows. Carl counted his cows and immediately jumped in his pickup and raced back over to Bulum's ranch. Upon his arrival at Bulum's, he was in a state of frenzy, continuously hurling new insults at Bulum with each mile traveled. By the time he arrived, he was so filled with fury that he leaped out of his truck before the truck came to a complete halt and cursed Bulum. "You bastard, where are my cafes?"

Bulum calmly restated the terms of their deal. I said I would return all the cows bearing your brand. Ranchers don't earn money from the process of fattening cows.

Ranchers desire for their cows to frequent as many cafes as possible. They want their cows to compound. Rancher's love "Horny Cows".

Rich people are money ranchers. They want their money to make them more money 24 hours a day. They want "Horny Money".

Poor people are like cowboys; they swap time for money. I do not want to talk about swapping time for money. Like Mathew said, "I knew you are a hard man, harvesting in places where you have not sown and gathering in places where you have not scattered seed."

I spent 10 years as a securities broker. I was fed a lot of industry Kool-Aid by the “vender trainers.” I learned from the securities companies that only uneducated individuals invested in things offering guaranteed interest, such as CDs. The potential for higher returns in higher risk mutual funds was evident, with an average that could reach 12%. Low risk equaled low return. The banks never disclosed to me the possession of a secret weapon, the ability to invest money at low risk and generate substantial returns. Returns that diminish the significance of what I just demonstrated, making it seem as small as a drop in the ocean. ...but the Rule of 72 accounted for only a small portion of what they were doing. Later I will show you that big lie, but first I’m going to show you the answer to low-risk high returns. Is it possible for the average person who despises debt to fight fire with fire? Wouldn't achieve poetic justice be possible by utilizing the very element that has kept you in poverty to bring you wealth? The Scottish people possess a saying “Hair of the Dog”. They held the belief that by rubbing some of the hair of the dog that bit you on the bite, it would protect you from evil. With a simple understanding of how debt works, even those with limited assets and common sense can profit from the most historically lucrative financial endeavor - debt!

Einstein declared the significance of compound interest as the most formidable force in the universe, and he devised a concept known as the "Rule of 72" to substantiate his claim. However, both Einstein and I committed the same error. Being in the presence of such brilliant individuals fills me with joy. I strongly believed that the average American would find the financial means or desire to take part in the same activities as the bankers highly unlikely. The concept of bankers utilizing OPM (Other People's Money) never crossed my mind, as they lack personal funds.

I'll provide you with an example of my flawed mindset. As a securities broker, I wanted people to invest in mutual funds. To convince them, I created a presentation explaining why putting money in a bank is not a good idea. A mentor of mine, Peggy Cook once told me she never made a poor decision based on the information she possessed at the time, but she did reserve the right to change her mind if she gained better information. This is the reason she got married 5 times. When I came up with this Rule of 72 presentation, I already consumed, as mentioned before, "a lot of securities, corporate vendor training Kool-Aid" regarding the wisdom of investing in mutual funds. At the time I consumed the training with the same enthusiasm as the followers in Jonestown consumed Cool-Aid. I didn't realize the self-serving and unchanging nature of the situation. One concealed drawback of mutual funds is the presence of fees and expenses. While the fact remains that mutual funds offer professional management and diversification, investors often overlook the fees associated with these funds. Mutual funds charge various fees, such as expense ratios, sales charges, and management fees, and surrender charges, which can significantly eat into an investor's returns over time. Mutual funds were created so that clients can treat them similarly to bank CDs. Another drawback is the lack of control over investment decisions. When investing in mutual funds, investors relinquish control over individual stock selection and portfolio management to the fund manager. This lack of control can be frustrating for investors who prefer a more hands-on approach to their investments. Additionally, mutual funds can sometimes have limited flexibility, as they may have restrictions on when investors can buy or sell shares. This lack of liquidity can be a drawback for investors who may need access to their funds quickly. Overall, while mutual funds offer certain benefits, careful consideration of these concealed drawbacks is essential for investors before investing in them. When you invest in a mutual fund you are not the one who is planning your future. Do you know what someone else has planned for you? Not much. First of all, you put funds in a mutual fund or 401k when you don't know the person who will be making all the financial decisions. Now admit it, that's a little peculiar. You're being informed about the funds' past performance not indicating future performance and the potential loss of your principal. Now why would the government force them to put a warning on their products? Is it possible that the specific thing they're warning you about has occurred before? Is it possible that performing the action later will prevent you from claiming that they didn't clearly warn you if you lose money? We refer to it as CYA, (Cover Your Ass).

The yield the fund generates and the yield you generate are two different things. They deduct all their fees before paying you. The term used is net effective yield. They don't manage your money for free. Their fees are owned by them, even if a financial loss occurs, they simply subtract the loss from your principal.

In summary, you find yourself entrusting your hard-earned money to a complete stranger. They explore uncharted areas of investment. In this particular circumstance, safety nets are absent, tangible assets cannot be utilized to protect your investment, and to compound the issue, no avenue for recourse exists. You signed a statement acknowledging your understanding of the risk involved. You signed the document because you didn't want the broker to realize your true lack of knowledge. Banks have discovered a more effective method to reduce risk and utilizing this method is essential for you. So, get dressed in some of your old clothes and read on.

*****

Chapter 9

Amortization: The Secret Banks Have Kept From Us

I'm having a hard time telling you about amortization. I remember the time I told my wife some jokes. "My wife hates my jokes", but she proceeds to call her sisters and shares the same jokes with them later. I ask her; "**What** starts with F and ends in K?" she told me, **"No it doesn't."** Getting what she said took me a few seconds, but I did feel a little dumb. (In case you're as dense as me; **What** starts with a "W".) I believed the answer would be Firetruck and I could coax her into saying a dirty word. To recover my pride, I ask her; "What's ½ of 20 plus 30? She fell into my trap and said, "40. I smiled and informed her of her mistake, following which she revisited my question. I smiled and asked her what's 20 plus 30?' She said "50." OK, what's ½ of 50? She punched me in the arm and called her sister. Both jokes helped me understand amortization. In both cases, the two answers were correct, but one was truer than the other. Consequently, I was compelled to provide a straightforward explanation of why my new response is more accurate than the previous one.

Banks have figured out a better way to mitigate risk. Amortization is a highly profitable mathematical formula, even more so than compound interest. However, I am not aware of any books that explain the specific mechanism. You won't receive any instruction about that during your college years. Lenders make huge profits that until now were beyond comprehension. In plain words, the lender charges what I call "Wallet Money. Wallet money is the actual amount of money that comes out of your wallet no matter what the contract says. They easily charge you over 100% interest while having you sign a contract that states that you are only paying 6%. They even make you sign something they call “Truth in Lending”. Truth In Lending fails to disclose the secret formula of amortization, making it far from truthful. I’m pretty good a math and even though they showed me the formula ($A = P\frac{i(1+i)^n}{(1+i)^n - 1}$) I still don’t comprehend what it’s telling me. Amortization guarantees them profit hundreds of times what they make off compound interest. They shield their "Wallet Money" rates in something legal, amortization, which allows them to circumvent most usury laws. They exploit the "Truth in Lending Laws" to conceal the truth.

*****

Chapter 10

Invest In Debt: It’s a Growth Industry

Throughout history, more money has been made from debt than from any other human endeavor, including all combined profits from gold, diamonds, real estate, stock market, big industry, oil, and lemonade stands. It was only in 1930 that amortization came into existence, and since then, more money has been made than in any other period of human history. Surprisingly, with this easy-to-understand fact, most people do not invest in debt. Few people even question the conventional wisdom that has been ingrained in them since they were young. You know what I'm talking about. The only way to make your money grow is to invest in the stock market or real estate or gold, your own business, etc. I know it's hard to be the person who says "the emperor is naked" but the emperor is naked. The answer to making good financial decisions and feeling in control of your own future is just to use your common sense. With a good dose of common sense, you will be able to convert this learning experience into decisive personal gain and avoid a dirt clod between the eyes.

Shakespeare said, "Neither a borrower nor a lender be" but Shakespeare was a writer, not a businessman. When the first entrepreneur grasped the "Principal of Collateral," the world started spinning faster. The "Principal of Collateral" encompasses a single uncomplicated rule, which has resulted in debt becoming the most profitable of all money earners. Collateral provides assurance to the lender that their money won't be lost. In the history of humanity this invention was as big as the wheel. Which plan would you rather invest in? The statement suggests that "past performance is no guarantee of future profit, and you could lose your principal." Or, if you cannot repay the loan, we will seize your property that has a higher value than the amount we lent you? Simply put, never lend money unless collateral is worth more than the money lent is present, and never invest money unless collateral is available. Well, duh. Shakespeare was talking about lending to family and friends without collateral. Now, such actions can have a detrimental effect on your finances. Banks, however, do not lend to friends. In fact, if you get a basic understanding of how banks make money you will know almost everything you need to know about making money for yourself. It is possible for you to visit a bank with the most outstanding business idea in the world. The banker might even tell you, “That idea is the best I've ever seen,” but when you ask them about lending you the money, they will merely respond, “Sure, what collateral do you have?”

I got all my material together and started to write a book about how banks make money. I typed; “Banks lend people money at a fixed interest rate, fixed term and payments and secure the loan with a good LTV (Loan to Value). I realized that I fully explained everything you need to know about how banks make money in just one sentence. The book I wrote was the shortest one yet, and I included it here at no extra charge. I know I'm repetitive when I say this, but here is the information; Banks don't invest, period. As soon as you grasp the bank's straightforward method to generate income using this universal system and implement it to your finances, you will also earn money similar to a bank. Banks make most of their money off amortization, not compound interest. Amortization is a 500-pound gorilla in the room. Yet no one seems to comprehend the situation, but you will soon.

*****

Chapter 11

Banks

Many individuals opt to invest in assets that banks typically overlook, like gold, stocks, mutual funds, CDs, annuities, bonds, and real estate. Banks operate under a very unpretentious investment policy; they lend money out, get collateral for a good loan to value and get paid a fixed payment for a fixed term at a guaranteed interest rate (I know, there I go again). Banks don't purchase a portion of a company and hope for profitability. They don't let anyone they don't know make investment decisions for them in companies they have never even heard of. They don't see any value in purchasing lumps of gold and locking them up in a vault. Banks sell individuals CDs so they can obtain their money at a low cost and invest, utilizing their amortization formula. Banks would never even consider buying an annuity. They hate owning real estate with all its liabilities and risk. In fact, they don't even refer to real estate as REO Properties. Banks engage in the practice of lending money, but only if there is sufficient collateral pledged to ensure that they will be able to recover their funds. In other words, banks don't gamble; banks like a guarantee they will get their money back. Wouldn't you? The way they do that is by securing the loan with collateral. Banks don't secure their money with "Hope." Banks don't secure their money with past performances; they secure their money with hard assets. Jim Rohn, the great philosopher, once said, "If you want to become wealthy, study what the wealthy people do and do that." Ok, I misquoted him. What he said was "Study what poor people do and don't do that," but it didn't really fit my point as well. You will feel better if you secure your financial future with hard assets. The same investment strategy banks use to make their investment decision is the best strategy for you as well. Banks make a lot of money using amortization. Even though people don't acknowledge its presence, it is constantly operating in the background.

Let me show just how amortization works.

You borrow $100,000 on a house.

Your interest rate 6%

Your term is 360 months.

Your payment $600 per month.

Your payment is divided into principal and interest with $100 going to principal and $500 going to interest. This is a typical 30-year mortgage. For every $100 you spend in principal reduction you spend $500 in interest. You don't need a fancy calculator to figure out what the real interest rate is that you're paying; 500%. You will make 360 monthly payments of $600, resulting in a total of $216,000. The interest you paid amounts to $116,000 or 116% instead of 6%. That's how amortization works. So, to summarize the bank had minor risk because they only financed 80% of the value of the house. Their $100,000 investment will end up making them $421,000. ...on a house that had appreciated at 3% and would be worth $421,000. Now I hope you understand why every Christmas the banks all have enormous Christmas trees, and you can only afford a tiny little one.

*****

The Stock Market

Industry Kool-Aid

I spent 10 years as a securities broker. I was fed a lot of industry Kool-Aid by the "vender trainers." Securities companies educated me on the fact that only the uneducated invest in things like CDs, which offer guaranteed interest. The idea resonated with me because I was unaware of the possibility of achieving high returns with low risk. I'm uncertain if the individuals in the securities industry are aware of the; Low risk equaled low return. I learned from the annuities industry about the best place to invest, which was in annuities due to their guarantee. Well, everything ended up being complete BS. Later I will reveal to you a significant falsehood, but first I'm going to present you with the solution to low-risk high returns. Is there a possibility for the average person who despises debt to fight fire with fire? Wouldn't there be poetic justice if you had the ability to utilize the very element that has kept you poor to make you rich? The Scottish have a saying "Hair of the Dog" where rubbing the hair of the dog that bit you on the wound can provide protection from evil. All that is needed is an explanation of how debt works for anyone with minimum assets and common sense to profit from the historically most profitable financial endeavor ever witnessed, DEBT. Based on Robert Kiyosaki, the writer of Rich Dad Poor Dad, two types of debt are present. Bad debt refers to debt that causes a decrease in wealth, such as credit card debt, car loans, and more. This is the type of debt used to buy liabilities. Good debt is debt which enhances your wealth, like a loan for investment property or for purchasing equipment for your business, which will generate a return. This is the kind of debt used for purchasing assets. But Kiyosaki is wrong. Two types of debt are present. Bad debt is when you owe someone, and good debt is when they owe you. Now that you understand amortization I'm sure you will agree; it's the best way to make money.

Einstein said that "compound interest was the most powerful force in the universe" and he came up with something call the "Rule of 72."

This was a tool most financial advisers loved to use in order to convince you banks are the last place on earth you want to put your money. Rule of 72 states if you divided your interest rate into 72, it would indicate the time to double your money. So, if you invested your money at 3% and wanted to know how long it would take to double your investment, you would divide 3 into 72 and the answer would be 24 years. At a rate of 6%, the process would take 12 years, while at 12%, it would take 6 years. The earlier mentioned gold, which paid 3%, would take 24 years to double. I don't know how many 24-year periods you have left, but I bet the remaining count is not significant.

I wanted people to put their money into mutual funds since I was a securities broker, so I designed a presentation to show why people should not put their money in a bank. A mentor of mine, Peggy Cook once told me she never made a poor decision off the information she had at the time, but she did reserve the right to change her mind if she got better information. That's why she was married five times. When I came up with this Rule of 72 presentation, I already experienced being fed, as mentioned before, "a lot of securities, corporate vendor training Kool-Aid" about the wisdom of investing in mutual funds. At the time I fully embraced and absorbed the training like Cool-Aid in Jonestown. I didn't realize the extent of its self-serving nature and resistance to change. Once, while teaching classes in physics, Einstein was asked why the final exam questions were the same as the year before. His reply was typical Einstein; "The questions are the same, but the answers have changed." I shared with you that story so you could observe the evolution of my thought process and comprehend how I can utilize the same example to demonstrate two distinct things. The answer has changed. I hope I am changing the way you think as well.

*****

Chapter 13

My Old Rule of 72 Presentation

People are amazed when they learn banks guarantee the interest rate they pay, but they don't realize the high cost associated with that guarantee. They are charging you for the guarantee on the interest rate guarantee, and this information is completely hidden from you. I know the sentence may surprise you, but some simple math will prove the truth to you. If you were to put $2,000 in a bank that paid 3% in 24 years, you would have $4,000 and in 48 years you would have $8,000. I know 48 years to make $6,000 ($8,000 - $2,000 deposited) sounds like a long time. Like I mentioned, I'm unsure of how many 48-year periods remain in your lifetime, but that's the calculation. If the bank invested your money in an investment that paid them 12%.

If they paid you the $8,000 they owe you after 48 years, you can see that they charged you $504,000 for the 3% guarantee. The total amount comes to $10,500 per year or $875 per month over 48 years. The math behind the 3% guarantee will cost you $875 a month for 48 years. I refer to this as a charge because there is nothing preventing you from making money like a bank.

This presentation should show people they needed to get a higher return than any fixed product like CDs could offer. Most people do not have enough time left on earth to settle for no stinking 3% interest. My presentation aimed to persuade people to invest in mutual funds, potentially earning them an 8% return on their money. I believed that the opportunity for a favorable return on their investment outweighed the risk of running out of money before time ran out. Mutual funds averaged better than CDs. At the time I wasn't given all the information about ways of making 8%. So, I exercise my "Peggy Cook Right" to change my mind.

What I didn't anticipate when I wrote the presentation surprised even me. When I finally came to understand how banks make money, I was forced to give up on "that invest in mutual funds" approach and to search outside the conventional wisdom box for a simple common sense, proven way to make money "like a bank. If the possibility existed for you to invest your money in the same manner as banks and receive a guaranteed interest rate of 12%, opting for that would be preferable than investing in something labeled as "WARNING" like mutual funds. I dislike purchasing items with a warning label because the presence of a warning label suggests that whatever is being warned about is likely happening to many people.

The math in my presentation was accurate and easy to understand. I changed the way people thought about interests and angered them enough to change their financial strategy. The only thing I got wrong was the information I had at the time did not lead me to the best solution for my clients. I hope you can forgive me and understand that I wish to show you a better way to invest using guaranteed interest instead of the hope of a return. The only problem you are probably wondering about is where I can get 12%.

*****

Chapter 14

How Compound Interest Works

To quote Shakespeare.

There is a tide in the affairs of men,

Which, taken at the flood, leads on to fortune;

Omitted, all the voyage of their life

Is bound in shallows, and in miseries.

On such a full sea are we now afloat?

And we must take the current when it serves,

Or lose our ventures.

The Things That Stop Us From Acting

The chance presented itself for me to ride my dirt bike in the desert west of town, which was one of the great things about Albuquerque. One day I was out by the Puerco River riding next to a dry gorge when something caught my attention. I observed what initially appeared to be a desiccated deceased cow at the base of the ravine, but then the lifeless cow shifted upon hearing my engine. I paused and observed the cow for a minute, attempting to understand what its issue was. The cow looked like she was dying of thirst, yet the river was only 150 yards away.

There was only one way out of the gorge and that was at the river. I had been playing in the bright clear water only a few minutes earlier, so I knew it wasn't dry. I rode off a small cliff and down into the gorge. I tried to shoo the cow to the water, but as we got closer, the gorge narrowed to about 4 feet wide. The wind blew approximately 5 or 6 tumble weeds into the narrow part, causing them to become stuck. Apparently, that unfortunate cow didn't believe she had the ability to push 5 or 6 10 oz. tumble weeds out of her way and turned to me and charged in the wrong direction. In my perception, I appeared less intimidating than 5 or 6 tumble weeds. I know she was not a bull, but when a 300-pound cow charges, you become a

Bull Fighter and step aside. After that, I went down to the tumbleweeds and moved them out of the way, which only took a few seconds. Afterwards, I returned to my foolish friend. I got her back to the same spot, and she stopped again. This time, she was extremely exhausted, only staring at me with those large sorrowful cow eyes and refusing to budge regardless of my screaming or arm-waving. I looked around for a stick or something you prod her with, but all I found was a dirt clod. I took that dirt cloud and with a light throw hit her right between those big brown, stubborn eyes. She wheeled around and took off running to the river. By the time I got back to my bike she was ankle deep in the river making a loud sucking sound.

I believe that sometimes we act just like that cow. We let five or six conventional wisdom tumble weeds to stop us from using our common sense. I promise I won't hit you between the eyes with a dirt clod unless I must. Don't make me have to.

*****

Chapter 15

Mutual Funds

Before I take you on a tour of how the financial industry makes money, I want to show you in new, easy-to-understand terms how mutual funds work. Most, if not all, the money you contribute into your 401k is invested in mutual funds. When you put money in a mutual fund, you are hiring a manager to buy small pieces of a lot of companies. You hope he or she is great or lucky at picking companies to buy shares in. You then own a small piece of those companies. If those companies generate profits, you receive a portion of the earnings deducted from the fees imposed by the mutual fund company for selling the shares and overseeing your investments. If any of the companies experience financial loss, then it diminishes the value of your shares. The money you earn when you invest in mutual funds, or the stock market is based on the earnings of the companies. Since accurate prediction of a company's profitability is impossible, a return cannot be guaranteed. Look at Bud Lite and Disney. They show the ever-changing nature of things. Mutual funds don't pay interest they pay a return. Returns can't be guaranteed, but interest can.

Most of the money in circulation makes many trips through banks and banks use their secret formula to make a profit on every penny.

Common sense will reveal the best course of action if you desire to make money is to learn from the strategies employed by the highest money earners and replicate their success. The biggest money earners by far are the banks.

Following countless repetitions of this presentation, I experienced an epiphany. Suddenly a realization struck me that instead of putting money in an aggressive high-risk mutual fund, risk adverse people should simply invest their money the same way banks do. Envision the increased amount of money you would possess presently and in the coming years if every penny that you had ever saved or invested in a 401k had earned a guaranteed 12%. Remember, it would double every six years. That's not even counting what you would make off the amortization. If you had invested $100 a month into something that provided a guaranteed 12% return for 20 years, your current balance would be $100,000. I venture to guess you don't have $100,000. I'm about to show you how to harness this powerful force for your own future. Envision the sensation of being able to smile even in times of market decline.

Who, in your opinion, earns the highest income? Do you believe it's the brokerage firms, insurance companies, real estate investors, or banks that sell stocks? The answer is the banks or any lender.

*****

Chapter 16

How Banks Make Money

The conventional wisdom is banks make their profit from lending out other people's money and charging a fixed interest rate. Well, that statement is only partially true. For you see banks do not really care what the interest rate is. Banks make the same profit from all mortgage interest rates, regardless of whether the rate is high or low. Banks make the same amount of money charging 3% as they do charging 9%. I know it's against what you would expect. I mean, how can it possibly be? Well, it's due to the fact that banks generate their income from the margin. Let me attempt to explain how they actually earn their money. If the bank is charging 4% interest on a loan, and the bank only pays 1% for the money it lent you. The cost of their money is 1%, like in a CD, then the bank is making 3% margin. If the bank is charging

9% interest, this is because they paid 6% for the money and they're making 3% interest. Competition keeps the margin competitive. Banks make a 3% margin on the interest, which is not bad, but their growth did not come solely from making a measly 3% off your money. They got rich because they understood **amortization** and you didn't.

Banks make money from something most of us have never even thought of as a profit generator even in our wildest imagination. This huge profit machine that banks have hidden from even the financial experts is called amortization; that's right. The way we pay the banks back is how they make the biggest part of their profit. Amortization is simply the math they used to calculate payments on all mortgages. With amortization, banks have the opportunity to gather a much larger amount of interest than principal during the initial ¾ of the loan. A certain rule in the mortgage industry, known as the "Rule of 50/25," is never openly discussed. The rule indicates that once you have paid 50% of the payments, your balance has only decreased by 25%. Does this sentence not indicate an interest rate of over 3%? Remember "Wallet Money. Banks use the 3% to cover their fixed costs like employees, buildings, 401 (k) and interest on their deposits. So, throughout history, banks have been able to hide what is possibly the most secure and profitable method of making money.

Now let's examine "the man behind the curtain" and comprehend the surprising truth of how the big money is generated and who generates it. To gain an understanding of amortization, let's examine a 30-year 6% mortgage of $50,000 with monthly payments of $300, belonging to a friend of mine. Don't let the math scare you. This is simple stuff. Like a child fearing the monster under the bed, we often fear math, but the lights can make the fear fade. Here is how a mortgage is broken down into easy-to-understand unpretentious math. Let's turn on the light.

A typical 30 year:

- $50,000 Mortgage
- 6% Interest
- $300 Payment

$300 Payment Breakdown:

- $250 went to interest (bank's profit)
- $50 went to principal reduction

To calculate the bank's profit margins from the 1st payment (divide principal into the interest) $50 divided into $250 = 5 or 500%. Let's break down the $300 payment. The $50 amount allocated to the principal is the bank recuperating their cost. Over the next 30 years, they will get their $50,000 back through the principal reduction from each payment. If the borrower refinances the house or sells the property, the principal is reduced from the balance owed by the small amount that has been applied. The $250, however, is interest, which signifies the bank's profit they never refund, even in the case of early loan repayment. So, let's do some simple math. If the bank's cost is $50 and their profit is $250, the bank's profit margin is 500%. For every $1 the bank collects in principle it collects $5 in interest on this $300 payment. This is again "Wallet Money", no matter what the contract says your wallet tells you the truth.

Now that you understand how banks make money, I want to ask you a question. Why do you think Einstein said, "compound interest is the most powerful force in the universe?" The only reason I can see why he made that statement was he didn't understand amortization. It's not that he couldn't comprehend it, but similar to the rest of us, he embraced conventional wisdom.

500% Is a Mighty Fine Return on Investment.

The return on investment is impressive, especially since it is backed by a hard asset with a great LTV (loan to value). The longer the borrower keeps the mortgage note the worse the bank's return gets. The average owner refinances or moves every 5 to 7 years, so the banks still make over 300% profit. The worst-case scenario is if my friend goes for the whole 30 years, then the bank makes $1.16 in interest for every $1 of principal paid (116%). So much for 6%.

I'm not stating that anything illegal or immoral is involved in the way banks make money, ultimately, it's just math. What I'm saying is wouldn't be fantastic if you could earn money that way? Wouldn't you like your investments to receive double digit interest with a fixed payment, which is guaranteed by collateral?

Let's approach the situation with a dose of common sense, shall we? Banks don't invest in the stock market; it's too risky, why should you? Banks don't buy annuities or save money inside life insurance policies because they see no financial logic in those investments, why would you? They don't buy real estate because they don't like the contingent liability of paying property taxes, maintenance, or property insurance, why would you?

In fact, banks hate real estate so much they don't even refer to it as real estate. They call it REO (real estate owned). Banks do something that is very simple; they lend people money at a fixed interest rate with a fixed payment and term. They guarantee themselves against loss with collateral at a good LTV (loan to value) of 80% to 90%. So, if the property is worth $100,000 they will only lend a maximum of $80,000 to $90,000. They receive their payments, or they take the collateral and sell the item. That is what I refer to as a sure thing.

What I'm getting at here is the reason banks don't invest in stocks, mutual fund, gold, or real estate. The commonsense answer is a question. Would you, armed with your current knowledge about how debt works, still consider investing in something else? Would you prefer to invest in something with a guaranteed 12% interest that is backed by collateral worth more than your initial investment, or in something with no guarantees?

*****

Chapter 17

Shelter From the Storm

Here are four compelling reasons you should transfer your money out of the stock market. In the movie "The Perfect Storm" three major storms all came together to form the perfect storm. Because of the combinations of temperatures, the jet stream, humidity and the season of the year, this storm grew unchecked until the storm destroyed everything in its path.

The sailors who ignored the warnings of disaster died for their arrogance whereas the sailors who took shelter from the storm survived.

I believe we are witnessing the gathering of not three major storms, but four major storms that, when they combine will become synergistic (more powerful than the sum of their parts).

The stock market experiences an increase, followed by a decrease. There is a possibility that you can earn good money when the market is on the rise, but you may lose it again when it declines. That might not scare you, but you need to understand that even though you made your money back on the upswing, you can't make up the time you lost. The trouble with time, unlike money, you can't get any more. many bubbles have impacted the market in the last few years. To give a few examples, the Tech Bubble and the Real Estate Bubble, along with the Inflation Bubble, have occurred. How many of these bubbles have you been through and continued to invest in the market? My dad liked to ask what he called learning questions, and one of his favorites was, “What do you learn the second time you are kicked by a mule?” He would always answer his own question quickly with, “Not a DAMN THING!” I know the last time the market dropped you swore you would never go through that again and yet here you are once more at the edge of a precipice, trying to brace yourself against the fall.

It is wise to take a moment to pause, allowing the sights and sounds of the situations that to are affecting your world, before engaging your common sense and redirecting your investments. Invest in something you can truly comprehend, rather than being swayed by someone else's sales pitch, and remember that in baseball nobody swings at every pitch. Use your common sense. Direct your gaze towards the man behind the curtain. I promise to not only guide you to a haven amidst this colossal storm but also reveal the precise methods to benefit from it. Hear the thunder crackling ominously and see the dark clouds looming overhead. Feel the cold gusts of wind brushing against your skin, carrying the scent of impending rain. Trust me, I will show you the way to survive and thrive in this the coming storm.

*****

Chapter 18

Baby Boomers

In the aftermath of WWII, servicemen returned home from the war, promptly getting married and initiating a baby boom, which led to approximately 10,000 newborns each day, lasting for almost twenty years. Babies born from 1946 until 1964 were called "Baby Boomers." Baby Boomers will influence your finances no matter how old you are. Like a snake with a basketball in its belly, the Baby Boomers glide through time, leaving a noticeable bulge in their wake. That bubble affects everything around it because like it or not, today everything is tied together.

Industries catering to this economic phenomenon have consistently thrived, while industries failing to acknowledge the shift in consumer demographics have faced extinction. You can measure the effect it has on all businesses. By 1964, these Baby Boomers were entering the workforce at a rate of about 10,000 a day. During that era, the prevailing practice among companies was to provide what is commonly referred to as defined compensation (Pension), ensuring a predetermined monthly sum upon retirement (defined benefit).

The industry faced significant pressure to expand and increase its workforce in response to the escalating demands from the rapidly growing population. These industries became aware that if they were hiring thousands of individuals per month at a certain point, an equal number of individuals would begin retiring per month.

In 1978, the 401k was specifically invented to enable companies to reduce their fiduciary cost (cost they were unable to avoid) of pension plans. The realization hit companies that if they continued with these plans, the exorbitant costs would lead them to bankruptcy, unable to sustain paying a significant workforce for not working. They came up with what is called 401k, "defined contributions" in which the company would set up a system where the employees could invest in the stock market and the company would match a percentage of whatever was invested. This system relieved the companies of the contingent liabilities of a pension plan. If employees contribute money to the plan, the company will also contribute, but non-contributing employees have no obligation to receive company contributions. The companies cut their expenses dramatically, resulting in significant cost savings. With a deep understanding of human psychology, they predicted that their employees would be reluctant to donate large sums of money, leading to minimal matching funds. When these Baby Boomers retired, the companies had no future obligations to worry about and no expanding expenses or fiduciary expenses (An expense they could not escape).

*****

Chapter 19

The Perfect Storm

In the movie "The Perfect Storm", three storms converged to create the perfect storm, a storm greater than all its tribe. This is the beginning of the first storm. In our history, the typical American had no experimented with the stock market. Only individuals with financial means were able to purchase mutual funds due to the high minimum investment required ($2,500 to $5,000) to initiate a mutual fund. When the mutual fund managers learned that 300,000 auto workers wanted to invest around $100 to $150 per month each they changed the rules to allow small initial investment. The employers agree to deduct the monthly $100 to $150 from the employee's paycheck before the taxes are paid. So, the employees were deferring taxes until they retired. This was the fuel that ignited the American economy. Every day, 10,000 new baby boomers flooded into the workforce, bringing with them a surge of investments in the market that lasted for 18 years. That's 3,650,000 new investors entering the market every year and very few people pulling their money out to retire; the workforce was young and the ones that were retiring already had a pension (defined benefit plan). There were millions and millions of people putting their money in the stock market. This was a novelty in the stock market, triggering an unprecedented economic boom that the world had never experienced.

Fast forward and see if you can predict the results of 10,000 baby boomers reaching retirement age every day and they will start taking their money out much faster than they put it in. Keep in mind, most retirees during this period still received pensions and did not withdraw funds from the stock market. However, each year the percentage increased significantly until the last eight years of the Baby Boomers, when almost all retirements depended on 401ks. The companies' fiduciary responsibilities began to shrink as the retires died off.

The companies will not suffer when the employees start removing the money from their 401ks but the stock market will. The economy will initially be able to handle these withdrawals, but soon the economy will be overwhelmed. The mutual fund managers have spent their whole life getting that automatic check from all the 401k companies. They possessed the capability to directly compensate departing individuals from the monthly deposits, bypassing the necessity to sell shares. The influx of money into the stock market eventually reached its peak and began to dwindle. Every day, 365 days a year, thousands of people retire, creating a symphony of clicking keyboards and rustling paperwork as they withdraw funds from their 401ks and IRAs. The fund managers will be left with no choice but to sell shares in order to provide the retirees with their monthly retirement check. As the volume of sell orders grows, that pulls the prices down of shares, thus forcing the mutual fund managers to sell more shares to pay people's retirement money. Mutual fund managers had developed a dependency on the consistent influx of money coming in. They seldom had to sell shares to pay people their retirement checks, but things have changed. A typical Baby Boomer has been putting $150 a month in his 401k for 30 years. The mutual fund manager has never experienced the pressure to sell shares during market downturns, thanks to the steady stream of deposits pouring in from 401ks. However, let's crunch the numbers and envision the future scenario when millions of Baby Boomers retire. Picture the manager overwhelmed with the task of accommodating monthly withdrawals of $3,000. The magnitude of this situation looms, filling the air with a sense of urgency and the smell of financial responsibility for which he has no escape. It will take 20 Millennials, putting in $150 a month just to equal the one Baby Boomer taken out $3,000. At some point, more money will flow out of the market than it flows in. At that point the mutual fund manager will have to start selling shares to pay the withdrawals. The more shares these mutual fund managers sell the lower the prices per share.

Before the Baby Boomers entered the market, when the market was down, people wanted their money out of the market, so managers had to sell the shares and got little chance to capitalize on a down market to purchase shares cheaply. When the Baby Boomers hit the stock market, managers knew how much was coming in every month and it wasn't affected by the market slowdowns. At one point, because of the steady influx of cash every month mutual fund managers profited from a dropping market. ... experts were unable to provide an explanation for its whereabouts. Well, the funds were allocated to support Baby Boomers during retirement. Because of the rising taxes on individuals with substantial savings people will be forced to withdraw larger amounts of money to meet their tax obligations. I'm sure you see the dramatic effect this will have on the market once the tipping point is reached. I call this, **"The Negative Drawdown Horizon**". I believe it is important for you to know, even though the securities industry would prefer me to remain quiet. I paid an exorbitant price for being the;" Whistle Blower".

Now you may say that the stock market is up because ten years ago the market value was at 20,000 and today the value stands at 39,000. That looks impressive, that's about a 6% increase in ten years but you're not factoring in inflation. If inflation was just 3% (It's up a lot more) then the market is only up 3%. That's not much of a return.

*****

Chapter 20

Storm Two: Withdraws For Retirement

In 2020, the outward tide speeds up because of the IRS rules on 401k. While drafting the rules for 401ks, the IRS expressed concern about individuals keeping their money in their IRA or 401k for an extended period, potentially hindering the government's ability to collect deferred taxes. To address this, they implemented a regulation to ensure the payment of deferred taxes. They wanted your money now. At first, the IRS came up with a rule called Mandatory Distribution, which required people to start withdrawing from their qualified plan at age 70 ½. Failure to start withdrawing funds at 70 ½ would cause a 50% tax. After careful consideration, they decided to make it perfectly clear that you must start taking your money out of your non-Roth 401ks or IRAs, so they changed the name to Required Mandatory Distribution. What this implies is that even individuals who haven't retired by age 70 ½ must initiate withdrawals or else. Baby Boomers will start hitting 70 ½ by 2016 and continue for 18 years at about 10,000 per day. If a storm with a massive tidal wave attached isn't present, I'm not certain what else it could be. You may have the impression that the government will modify that law and not require people to withdraw their funds. That can never happen; the government actuaries have estimated to the penny exactly how much tax revenue the distributions will generate, and Congress has already spent that money. Regardless of your age group, if you possess investments in the stock market, you'll observe your share values plunging rapidly. No matter what you believe, we are all united in this journey. With this negative cash flow, capital investments for the future will become very expensive and that will put another drag on the economy along with the inflation that it will carry with it.

*****

Chapter 21

Storm Three: Higher Taxes

When we began investing money into our 401ks and IRAs, we were informed that we would be postponing the taxes when our tax bracket is high due to having income, to a time when our tax bracket would be low as our income decreases during retirement. How many of you believe our taxes are decreasing? You should consider the scenario if taxes were to rise. So, what we did was defer the taxes when they were low to a time when they were high. If the taxes are higher on the money we withdraw, we must pull out more money. I know that I'm redundant. The mutual fund manager must sell more shares to send out those retirement checks. The cost of shares goes down because there are more sellers than buyers. The retirees will have to withdraw more and more money to maintain their already diminished lifestyle. At some point the government will have to stop printing money as it is now to cover this outflow. Are you beginning to see a pattern? Since I can't figure out how the current system can continue, I suggest that your plans include the scenarios I am predicting. More money coming out of the stock market and withdrawals speeding up faster and faster each year has got to impact your finances.

*****

Chapter 22

Storm Four: Student Loans

I heard on the news yesterday about 7 out of 10 college graduates having student loans of approximately $30,000. When we Baby Boomers graduated college, our parents may have had less wealth, but we were not burdened by any debt. We got married, started a family, got a job, and bought a house. This time was called the "Housing Boom. We possessed the income to purchase and sustain a house. Today when college graduates get out of school they need to get a job and start paying their student loan back. This indicates they are delaying marriage. Marriages are happening later and later so they don't need a house. Home purchases are nearly unattainable for young adults, not just due to the high interest rates but also because qualifying is challenging given the debt-to-income ratio imposed by student loans. Not only will saving for a house be challenging for the millenniums, but the Dodd Frank law also renders banks uninterested in providing loans under $100,000, thus making small loans obsolete. Dodd-Frank was meant to prevent the excessive risk-taking that led to the financial crisis. But what it did was take away the financial advantage for banks to take risk on

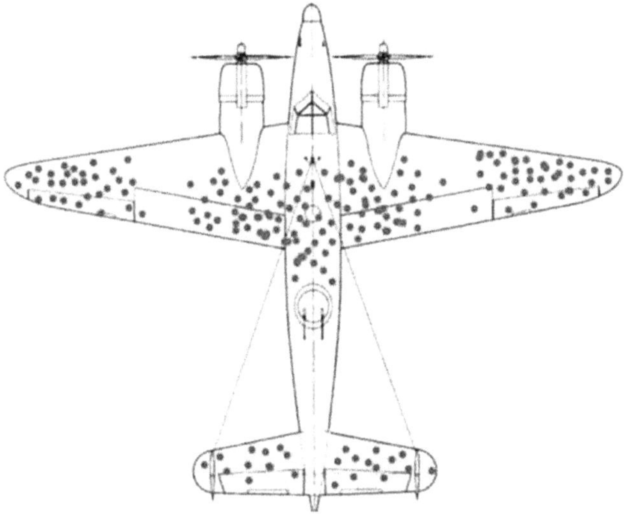

small loans.

I witnessed an instance of incorrect thinking on the internet. In WWII the British marked where most planes were hit. They wanted to know so they could strengthen those spots.

But one individual (Abraham Wald) instead argued that the parts unaffected were the ones that needed protection.

He explained that what they saw were only the planes returning to base, not the ones shot down. The planes that were hit in the white spots (untouched, in the graph) had not returned home and therefore had not entered their apparently flawless reasoning. Therefore, the LEAST AFFECTED areas of the graph had to be strengthened. And he was right. This story, once again, reminds us that the road to hell is paved with good intentions. And that information and intelligence, without the KNOWLEDGE AND ABILITY TO INTERPRET DATA, make people commit terrible bullshit.

Dodd Frank limits the amount banks can charge on small loans. This will influence the housing industry. Who will be the buyers for new homes? Rental property will become a premium.

Another consequence of this debt will be young adults who are paying off student loans unable to save for their retirement. This alone will lower the amount of money going into the market and severely delay their savings for their retirement, and when you add in their increased cost for health insurance, the death spiral steepens. Thank you Obama Care.

Had enough gloom and doom?

*****

Chapter 23

The Bright Side of the Road

Depressed yet? Throughout the rest of this book, I will guide you on your journey to find the way out. A way to escape the death spiral stock market and prosper. If you are already investing in real estate, it is likely that you had a premonition of the imminent storm that will devastate the stock market and you have placed your trust in something that is supported by collateral. This market decline is self-fueling and as it touches, many other industries too will suffer. For instance, insurance companies base their ability to pay a return on their annuities on their investments in the stock market. I can't imagine young people continuing to put their money in a market that loses money year after year. Next you'll learn how to make money like a bank.

*****

Chapter 24

Investing In Debt for the Average Person

The very first thing to do is to redefine your approach to making money. From now on, use your God given common sense to make financial decisions and forget all that failed conventional wisdom nonsense. Let's look at some good old common sense secret investment strategies that the highest money earners used to make money.

I want to talk about not only how banks make money, but how you can do the same thing. When a bank lends money for a house that is called a mortgage. When an owner finances a house, the process is referred to as a mortgage note. To comprehend the meaning of a mortgage note, simply remove the word "note." When you buy a mortgage note, you become the bank. Banks generally will lend about 80% to 90% of the value of the home depending on 2 things; the borrower's ability to pay which they use a credit score to determine and or any government program that will cover any loses if they lend you the money at a low ratio (90% to 100% of value). Because banks can't competitively only finance 40% or 50% of the value, they look to other factors than LTV to secure their loans. So, they invented credit scores. The higher your credit score the higher LTV they will lend.

People have been offering, owner finance for years. These individuals own a house and offer to finance it themselves. Because of the new Dodd Frank banking rules banks don't like to do small mortgage loans because the new law will not let them make much money. Banks work just as hard to do a $90,000 loan as they do to do a $900,000, except they make little money on the small loans. Because banks don't prefer to engage in small loans, finding a buyer who can qualify through a bank is extremely challenging due to the banks' strict adherence to inflexible high standards for credit scores. Banks also dislike lending to people who own their own business. The bank will eliminate most of the likely buyers, which can stretch the time on the market forever. Why would someone who owns a house be willing to take on the risk of doing the financing themselves, well if they owner finance there are a lot more prospective buyers and as you just read the 500% profit margin mean the seller/financier makes more money, but it doesn't cost the home buyer anymore? I summarize banks make a lot of money doing big mortgages but they have moved away from small loans. This has opened a gigantic profit opportunity for the average American to invest in debt and buy small mortgage notes.

Allow me to provide you with an illustration of what exactly a mortgage note entails and what the wallet money is. The homeowner wants to sell the house she inherited from the death of her mother for $100,000. If someone wants to buy it and can qualify at a bank for a loan, the bank will lend them $90,000 and make the buyer put $10,000 down. At closing the seller must pay a real estate agent 6% or $6,000 and maybe some other charges. So, the seller gets about $94,000. What the owner would like is a steady cash flow from the property, but she doesn't want to mess with renters. If she would just advertise "House for sale, no qualify owner finance" the buyers will beat a path to her door. She gets $10,000 down and finances the house for 20 years at 6% with payments of $716.43 a month. In 10 ½ years she has collected $100,000, $10,000 down and $90,000 in payments and the buyer still owes her another $81,673 or 114 payments of $716.43. Multiply 114 payments times $716.43. If she sold the house and the bank financed it, she would only get $94,000, but if she owner financed it she gets $182,000; the payoff and the payments she already got. The homeowner pays the same either way, but if the original owner does owner/finance, she makes an additional

$96,000 instead of the bank reaping the benefits. The scent of opportunity lingers in the air as the homeowner contemplates the financial possibilities. The sound of money being saved echoes through her mind, like a symphony of financial success. The sight of dollar signs dances before her eyes, fueling her determination to seize this chance. A sense of empowerment envelops her, acknowledging that she has the ability to seize control of her financial future. The statement suggests a conflict between conventional wisdom and common sense in a particular situation. It implies that what is traditionally accepted as wise or logical may not align with what is intuitively sensible or practical. Carl Sagan said, "We simply accepted what the most widely available and accessible source of information claimed is true. For our naiveté we are systematically misled and bamboozled." Don't be bamboozled

*****

Chapter 25

Benefits of Mortgage Notes/Real Estate Notes

When you buy a mortgage note no property is being purchased, no rehab is needed. Since no property is being purchased, you don't pay property taxes. Finally, as a note buyer, you are not a landlord; rather, you are the note holder (Lienlord'), and you are not responsible for any of the maintenance or wear and tear that happens to the house.

*****

Chapter 26

Shelter From the Storm

So how do discount mortgage notes give you shelter from the storm?

1. In a mortgage note, your money remains detached from the unpredictable ebbs and flows of the stock market. Therefore, the rollercoaster ride of stock market fluctuations holds no sway, allowing you to navigate your financial journey with tranquility.

2. The sight of people swiftly withdrawing their money from the bustling stock market, accompanied by the frantic sound of transactions, has no bearing on the monthly mortgage payment that you receive.

3. As a note holder, you have the power to shape your tax situation. One way to do this is by

utilizing a self-directed ROTH IRA within a qualified plan. Alternatively, if you opt for an unqualified plan, you will only be taxed on the interest paid, sparing the taxation of the principal. Take control of your financial future and make informed decisions.

4. In a bustling cityscape, where the sounds of hurried footsteps and honking cars fill the air, the sight of more people earning meager wages becomes akin to igniting the flames of the small mortgage note business.

5. Your money is tirelessly working, generating wealth every second of the day, every day of the week.

6. Rest assured; the strength of your investment lies securely within the tangible value of the property.

Using mortgage notes as part of your investment strategy is a logical choice. They act as a sturdy safety net amidst the ever-changing market, providing a sense of security. Moreover, they offer an enticing opportunity to reap the benefits of the real estate world, while skillfully avoiding its less favorable aspects. You can shop for mortgage notes on Google. Let me explain how they work. You should write these numbers down so you can see what I'm talking about.

Let's say a homeowner, named Bill, financed his brother, Tom, purchase of his house. The house is worth $200,000. Bill set up a mortgage for $200,000 for 30 years at 6% with payments of $1,200 a month. In 10 years, Tom still owes Bill $167,371. That $1,200 a month for 20 more years. ($1,200 X 240= $288,000) Bill decides that he wants his money now, so he offers to sell the $167,371 balance at a discount. The average discount is 20 to 30% or a $50,000 discount. If you purchased the mortgage for $117,371.

Tom would then owe you $167,371 or 240 payments of $1,200. This is the cool thing about buying that mortgage. The $200,000 house most likely appreciated at 3% making your collateral on your $117,371 investment $269,870 or an LTV of 57%. Now that's a great LTV. Because you bought it at a discount your interest rate is much higher than 6%. You're making 10.86% and you're taking advantage of amortization. The great thing about this is Tom's deal didn't change a penny, he still pays the same $1,200 a month for the same 20 years. The only thing that changes is you're making the profit.

Now we need to examine the four potential outcomes.

1. Tom stops making the payment. You foreclose and you get a house that is

probably worth more than $270,000. You sell the item and after deducting expenses, you make approximately $135,000 in profit.

2. Tom refinances the loan. The bank that gave him the loan will have to pay you the payoff of $167,371. Since you invested $117,371 your profit is $50,000.
3. Tom sells the house. You make $50,000.
4. Tom goes the next 20 years and pays off the mortgage. You made $1,200 a month for 240 months, that's $288,000 minus your $117,371 investment. You made $170,629 profit. You made a guaranteed 10.86% interest.

*****

Chapter 27

AN INDUSTRY IS BORN

The moment I unraveled this mystery, my eyes scanned the room, taking in the brightly lit surroundings. The sound of my own heartbeat echoed in my ears, the only noise breaking the silence. I was able to detect the aroma of hamburgers frying. I was in a Whataburger. A surgc of excitement ran through me as I connected all the pieces. I first became aware of the fact that most mortgages were sold at a discount when I became a mortgage broker. Nearly all the mortgages were resold quickly at a discount. If you ever purchased a house, chances are you received a letter in the first month notifying you that the original mortgage company had transferred your mortgage to another mortgage company. In the absence of an easily comprehensible guide on selling discount mortgages, I found myself compelled to unravel its intricacies through personal exploration.

I wanted to know how they made money by selling the mortgages. I understood amortization and thought making money didn't get any better than that. So, I used my trusty Texas Instruments, BA II, Walmart financial calculator for about $30 or at the App Store for free. I've experienced a few epiphanies in my life and this qualifies me as one of them.

Banks charge points to increase their upfront profit. Here is an example. The bank lends Joe $100,000 on a $130,000 valued house. Then charges him 4 points to do the loan or $4,000. Their gross profit is then $4,000 up front. They sell that $100,000 mortgage at a discount for $99,000 to someone who understands amortization. The discount mortgage buyer is getting 6.13% interest instead of the original 6% because of the discount. Recall the 500% profit margin? The bank previously had a profit of $4,000, but now they only have a profit of $3,000. So why would they do that? They possess a profit of $3,000 and managed to retrieve their initial investment of $100,000, which is the reason. Let's say they simply loan the same $100,000 out 4 times a month on other mortgages. So, their profit at the end of the specific month is $12,000. If they repeated those 4 times a month for a year, it would cause a profit of $144,000 on the same $100,000. You comprehend the reason behind my statement about having an epiphany. Understanding something seemingly straightforward completely transforms my beliefs about investing. I knew from that point on I needed to let the world know what a marvelous investment opportunity discount mortgage notes were.

This is the beginning of what will become a tremendous shift in how small mortgages are done. With the invention of credit scores, the process of obtaining financing on a house became increasingly difficult for young people. The government decided to stimulate the market and compelled lenders to give loans to individuals who were unable to afford them. As a result of the law of unintended consequences, a false market has been created by the new banking laws. The banks didn't care because the government was guaranteeing the loan. This and the banks' willingness to cheat with the value and quality of these notes (derivatives) caused the collapse of the housing industry. After the housing bust the banks swung back the other way and refused to do small loans. The government once again attempted to control the market and passed the Dodd-Frank Law, aiming to make the fees banks charged for a loan "fair". Of course, the law of unintended consequences made it impossible for a bank to justify their expenses to do a small loan, so they stopped doing them. Today, getting a small loan is extremely difficult.

Nature abhors a vacuum, and the owner finance industry was reborn. You have probably heard the ad on TV about "it's my money and I want it now." Well, many people who did owner/finance have decide that they want their money now and will sell their mortgage notes at a discount.

Here is an example of a note.

Term	240 months
Interest rate	9.9%
Borrowed	$26,500

Payments	$253.98
Payments made	9
Loan Balance	$26,171
Discount	$5,171
Note price	$21,000

(The way to calculate this note will be shown in the BAII Manual)

It is apparent that the original interest rate is 9.9% and the homeowner has a balance of $26,171. She will pay $253.98 a month for the next 231 months. You can buy this note for $21,000, which is a $5,171 discount. Your LTV will be 40% and the interest rate you receive is 13.4%. The reason your interest rate is higher than the owner is paying is because you would have purchased the $26,171 note for $21,000, a difference of $5,171. The homeowner has a contract to pay 231 more payments of $253.98. Since you only have $21,000 in the note, the interest rate you receive is higher than the note shows. The owner of the house doesn't see any difference they just mail their check to a different address. When you are figuring the price you should pay for this note, you need a discount it is enough to make it pay you at least

13% and it's guaranteed by the house, which is the collateral.

You can either purchase a Texas Instruments BA II Plus calculator from places like Walmart, which typically cost around $30, or simply download it for free from the Apps Store on your phone. That will be the best step you ever took; your return will be phenomenal.

As you can observe, this is even better than the way banks make money because when a bank grants a loan, it remains at that rate for them, but if you purchase a discounted note, your interest rate increases. It's somewhat difficult to comprehend, but I will show you how to do it in the free BAII Manuel. That's why buying a discounted mortgage note is so sweet.

*****

Chapter 28

WHY DISCOUNTED MORTGAGE NOTES ARE BETTER THAN RENTAL INCOME

A national reporter emailed me the other day and asked for my expertise on an article she was working on.

Query:

I need to talk to an expert on buying rental property. Is now a good time to purchase a low-end property with the purpose of renting out? What areas are best for rentals now? How long will the process take for you to recover your investment? Etc.

This was my response: "I would rather eat a pungent bowl manure soup than buy rental property".

When investing in income property, securing a loan can pose as a challenge. Hard money lenders typically require a substantial down payment, usually around 60 to 65% of the property's value. The terms; under 5 years with a balloon

• High interest rates and it's amortized.

• You pay for the maintenance

• Pay for the insurance

• You pay the property taxes, which will get higher and higher with this federal spending frenzy.

• People tear up things they rent

• You try to buy houses you would live in instead of houses that will make you money

• You are on call; toilets only stop up on Sunday when the Cowboys are playing.

• You will be lied to; the checks in the mail, the bank screwed up, there was enough money in my account to cover the rent check the bank screwed up and of course the old stand by my dog ate the check.

In my opinion, a standard old savings account will repay your investment sooner and you don't need a Plumber's Friend to buy a CD.

I asked an income property owner in Albuquerque how many houses he owned. To which he replied, "I don't know, but I do know I own 27 toilets. In my estimation, owning rental property is preferable to owning stocks, however, I am convinced that discount mortgage notes are even more favorable.

Why should you only do notes on low end property. During my childhood, I would eagerly embark on my annual pilgrimage to Longview, TX, to spend summers with my beloved grandfather. In retrospect, I now understand that every moment spent in his presence was a meticulously designed instruction, etched into my mind. Each interaction, each activity, carried with them a purpose, a hidden wisdom waiting to be unraveled. I called my grandfather Pop. Pop, the weathered patriarch, possessed an ancient, moss green Studebaker pickup, its verdant hue whispering tales of forgotten journeys and hard use. Much of its paint had been consumed by the sun. And the utilization of a pair of pliers was necessary to roll down the window. By contrast, his pristine white Cadillac stood regally, emanating an air of refined luxury. He claimed ownership of a collection of diminutive rent houses, their humble appearance reminiscent of modest shacks. Pop would bring me along in that old Studebaker truck without air conditioning to collect the rent payments, as he didn't want his tenants to perceive him as wealthy. He always made me be the driver, even when I was ten, because he enjoyed taking the whiskey bottle he concealed in the garage and sipping from it as we went on our rounds. I named that truck "The Money Vac" and the only purpose for which he used that vehicle was to collect payments, always in cash. He told me he had rather have 10 low rent houses than one high rent house. He mentioned that if the economy worsens, a significant demand for low rent houses would arise, and even if the economy improves, the demand for low rent houses would still be substantial. These houses were scattered all over Gregg County Texas. During my childhood, my father worked as a car salesman. Pop, explain the economics behind buying a car versus buying a house. He would emphasize that purchasing a car meant spending money, while its value would inevitably diminish over time. In contrast, investing in a house and renting out a property would cause a steady income stream and an increase in the property's value. I would say Pop had a good understanding of what he was discussing. I ask him if that was true why does he own such an expensive car? "I bought your grandmother that Cadillac because I got caught lying." He said with a slight smile. "I informed her I stopped drinking."

Then he said something that I didn't understand at the time; "A happy wife makes a happy life." He then smiled and took another sip.

Nowadays, many people acknowledge the truth in what Pop taught me. However, they struggle to make ends meet and never have sufficient funds to invest in income properties. Many spend thousands going to Rich Dad Poor Dad programs to learn how to buy income property, but few ever get it done. The property is hard to find close to where you live and expensive to finance. Just too many headaches come with being a landlord, but Pop still had a good idea. He knew that the collateral was good, and the residual income lasted a long time.

After exhausting all the "No Money Down Plans," you finally realize that venturing into the world of real estate can offer a more stable and profitable source of passive income. The sight of fluctuating stock market charts no longer entices you, as you yearn for the security and potential that real estate holds. The sound of whispers among successful investors fuels your desire to take the plunge. The smell of opportunity lingers in the air, enticing you to seize the moment. With your hard-earned money at stake, you long for the sense of reassurance that only real estate can offer or at least that's what you've been taught. Remember what Peggy Cook said, she never made a poor decision from the information she had at the time, but she did reserve the right to change her mind if she got better information. So, you need some better information.

The new paradigm is the purchase of mortgage note. Owner financed notes are becoming the best option to save for retirement because they offer a fixed interest rate on your money.

The good things are.

1. You are not the landlord you are the Lienlord, so you don't have to fix things.

2. You are the lien holder you don't pay property tax.

3. You don't pay for the insurance.

4. You don't pay maintenance.

5. You don't deal with many people moving in and out.

6. You get paid a fixed interest rate that's amortized.

7. Your money has a hard asset backing it at a good LTV.

8. Your taxes are lower because some of each of the payments is return of principal. You don't pay capital gains tax because it's interest income.

9. You can make this your Self-Directed IRA.

10. You can make this a savings type account.

11. If you must repossess it you can sell it again as owner/finance; there are always a lot of buyers with owner/finance.

13% Interest

Interest Can be Guaranteed but You Can't Guarantee a Return

There is a vast difference between interest and yield. The money you earn when you invest in mutual funds or the stock market is based on the earnings of the companies. Since it is impossible to accurately predict the profitability of a company, it is not possible to guarantee a return. Mutual funds or stocks and these types of investments don't pay interest they pay a yield. The two are not even calculated the same way.

Mortgage notes are, in reality, mortgages, and mortgage payments are calculated using a fixed guaranteed interest rate and term. The payments are guaranteed by the collateral. The payments are not connected to the profit of any company.

If the mortgage contract (note) you purchased has a fixed payment and term then it charges a guaranteed interest rate. In other words, you are paid a guaranteed interest backed by a hard asset.

*****

Chapter 29

Start Earning a High Fixed Interest Rate Today

As the golden years stretch longer, the ever-rising cost of living looms, casting a shadow over retirement dreams. The dwindling options for secure savings now lack the sweet promise of high returns, leaving a bitter taste of uncertainty in the air. Besides difficulties in saving for retirement, how do you keep the money you saved for retirement and how do you strategize if you lack a way of knowing what your return will be?

The following are some ‘conventional wisdom’ ideas on how to save and live through retirement:

A few people still have a Depression-era mentality when it comes to saving money and like to have the safety and security of a bank account. The downside to how banks really work is the low interest rates they pay for this service. Banks can currently borrow money from the Fed almost interest free, therefore, they don't need to pay consumers a high interest rate for their deposits. The money they borrow from the Fed is the same thing as the money they borrow from you in a CD or savings account. Most interest rates for savings accounts and even Certificates of Deposits are below the level of inflation. And what little interest they pay they are taking out in fees and charges. The banks persuade individuals to lend them money, offering a meager 1 or 5% interest, and then lend it out at significantly higher rates. These numbers move up and down but average about the same. Your money you get pennies, and they get the lion's share. How did they sell that to us? The answer does not lie in our lack of intelligence; rather, it lives within the realm of "Conventional Wisdom."

*****

Chapter 30

Why Mutual Funds?

Do you recall your initial impression when someone first mentioned mutual funds to you?

OK, let me get this straight; you spend the next 20 years giving some dude money every month, so when you are ready to retire he "may" give you back more money than you put in. What do you mean he is going to invest it and never even tell you in what? However, he is going to give you something he calls a prospectus that is as hard to read as a phone bill.

Can you visualize getting paid a guaranteed 13% when banks are only paying 1/2%? Most notes should be calculated so you make at least 13%. Unlike mutual funds, annuities, or stocks, it does not matter what the Dow Jones Industrial Average is. Low end housing is where most of the real estate market growth will come from. Small mortgages thrive in economic downturns because people can still afford to buy owner/finance property and when the economy gets bad people move down into lower-cost housing. This market is feed from the top and the bottom. Young people enter the real estate market from the bottom, individuals who experienced a loss of income enter from the top. Low end is the next growth market.

Many people have asked me "Why would anyone finance a home at 13%?" My answer is the fantastic part of mortgage notes; nobody finances the original note at 13% but 13% is what you as the buyer of a discount note receive. You can't guarantee a return in mutual funds but you can guarantee interest in a loan. Since mortgage notes are loans, the interest is guaranteed by the collateral. I enjoy having recourse on my money. If you had money in GM stock when GM declared bankruptcy you simply lost your money and you had no recourse. However, when it comes to mortgage notes, there is a means to regain your funds known as collateral.

This is counterintuitive, but the original interest rate has **nothing** to do with the interest rate you receive. You would think that the higher the interest rate the more money you would get every month but that has more to do with the terms of a note.

*****

Chapter 31

BA II Plus

Let me show you the math. Understanding this becomes easier with the possession of a $30 Texas Instruments BA II Plus calculator. Let's consider the note you are looking at was originally $100,000, at 0% for 30 years, with payments of $277.78 per month. The borrower has made 120 payments, and the payoff is $66,666. With 20 years to go. Sentence 1: You may wonder how it's possible to make money on a zero present loan. Well, here's the math. In your BA II, you would enter 240 on the 2nd (Number of remaining months). Enter 13 in I/Y (interest rate). The result will equal $23,709. You should buy this note for $23,709 to make 13%.

This example teaches you how to determine the price you will pay for a note. If the product doesn't yield a return of 12 or 13%, don't purchase it.

If you don't currently possess a BA II, simply trust me for now and when you have the opportunity, acquire one and verify my calculations.

The advantage for you becomes clear when you are comparing one note against another to see how hard your money is working for you.

Three Things That Can Happen in a Mortgage Note

1.) The homeowner stops making payments and you foreclose.

George Bernard Shaw once famously said, "If you can't eliminate the skeleton in your closet, teach the skeleton to dance." This insightful quote immediately brings to mind one of the most common concerns people raise when discussing mortgage notes: What happens if the homeowner suddenly stops making their payments? Well not only does this skeleton dance, but it dances very well.

Out of the three options, you may find it surprising that foreclosure is the most profitable outcome for you, the mortgage note holder. I know this is not intuitive but let me explain. These notes are at a GREAT LTV.

1.) Owner sells or refinances.

In the following example, the mortgage note is for $26,500 and 9.9% for 20 years. The value of this property was $52,000. The balance on the note if you bought this note was $23,565. There is a possibility that you could foreclose on the property if the owner never made a single payment, after purchasing the note for $21,000. You possess the sum of $21,000 in a house that you currently own. The house is worth $52,000. Literally hundreds of thousands of people in the United States at this very moment are searching for $52,000 houses that they could purchase.

This also gives you a chance to get a good down payment and owner finances the house yourself.

Smaller Notes Are Best

Many reasons exist for suggesting that you only purchase small notes of $50,000 and below. As I just mentioned, there are only 3 occurrences in a mortgage note. All of them are to your advantage. Your money grows faster if any of these three happen. Don't forget what I said about the value of time. The occurrence that happens most frequently is paying off early. This happens more often because the average American moves or refinances their house every 5 to 7 years. When you purchase the note, the individuals living in the house had already been there for a few years, resulting in a shorter average duration of your stay. When they move they sell the house and whoever buys it must pay you off to get the lien released so you would be paid the original amount amortized payoff. In other words, they must pay you the remaining balance of the original loan. The same thing is true if they go to a bank to refinance. Here is an example of the increase in yield you get if the previous note was paid off in 1 year. Example:

In 12 months, the payoff is $25,693, you have received 12 payments of $253.98 (12 X $253.98

= **$3,047.76**). You paid $21,000 for the note so your yield is 34%. You made $7,740 off of a $21,000 investment in 1 year.

This example shows the tremendous increase in your yield if they move or refinance. The best way to make this happen is to buy small notes so you will have more notes that could pay off early.

So, would this work just as well on a big note you ask? Well, yes, it would, but it increases the odds of someone moving or refinancing 4 times if you own 4 notes for $25,000 each instead of 1 note for $100,000. That's the same reason you don't just buy one lottery ticket.

In the movie The Hunger Games, before the games begin they always say, "May the odds be ever in your favor." You want to increase your odds of one or more of your notes paying off early because it increases your yield dramatically. The best way to stack the odds in your favor is to buy as many small notes as you can.

If you are saving the payments, you are getting each month soon you will have enough to buy another note. Buy notes from $10,000 to $50,000. It doesn't take long for you to buy another note. Then you would possess double the amount coming in each month and the time it took you to purchase the next note is reduced by half. Every additional note reduces the time required for purchasing another, and every early payment accelerates the process.

When I informed you that only 3 events occur in a mortgage, the one that occurs most frequently is early payment. My clients have made over 500 notes in the last 5 years and fewer than 10 foreclosures have occurred, so that's rare. I don't know many people who have stayed in the same loan and house for 15 years, so the odds of them moving or refinancing is the most likely. But again, foreclosure is generally profitable.

Guaranteed Interest

Securities brokers may not inform you about the guarantee of returns on mutual funds because it is uncertain whether they will be profitable or not. The best way to make money in the stock market is to only buy stocks that go up in value. The statement was simple to make but impossible to carry out. I have discovered that during conversations with securities brokers, they believe I cannot use the term guaranteed. However, you comprehend that mortgage notes are not covered by securities law and are classified as "Exempt Transactions."

Article 581-5. Exempt Transactions.

Except as in this Act specifically provided, the provisions of this Act shall not apply to the sale of any security when made in any of the following transactions and under any of the following conditions, and the company or person engaged therein shall not be deemed a dealer within the meaning of this Act; that is to say, this Act shall not apply to any sale, offer for sale, solicitation, subscription, dealing in or delivery of any security under any of the following transactions or conditions:

J. Wherein the securities disposed of consist exclusively of notes or bonds secured by mortgage or vendor's lien upon real estate or tangible personal property, and the entire mortgage is sold or transferred with all the notes or bonds secured thereby in a single transaction.

Notes all have a fixed interest rate, which is guaranteed by the real estate. By contrast this rate cannot change. That is meant by guaranteed interest rate as it applies to a mortgage note or a fixed rate mortgage. Since a fixed interest rate is provided, planning your future becomes easier.

I am no longer a securities broker, so all I can do is advise you to extract some information from the US securities website so you can determine for yourself if securities have excessive fees, charges, and uncertainty associated with them. As an X securities broker I can only tell you I would never put one red cent of my own money in a mutual fund, because I understand how they work.

*****

Chapter 32

Annuities:

With an annuity, you put money in an insurance contract that pays a fixed or variable rate of return and start receiving guaranteed payments. Many people like the guaranteed payments, and the safety associated with earning a guaranteed interest rate. But the fees associated with these plans, and the fact that you lose control of your principal when the policy 'annuities' when you receive payments makes this a horrible solution. The insurance companies put together 170+ pages of information for consumers, knowing that they will read nothing about all the fees and charges. "Small print leads to large expenses and a lot of print is used to camouflaging the truth." You must understand in finance the truth is the first casualty. To quote Jonathan Gruber, a professor at MIT and an architect of Obamacare, "**Lack of transparency** is a huge political advantage. And essentially, attribute it to the foolishness of the American voter." I know he was talking about the ACA but the same principals apply. The annuity company doesn't print the 170-page book to make YOU money they do it so you will not understand. The situation becomes excessively convoluted to comprehend when making a purchase, and excessively simple for others to bewilder you, leading you to depend on conventional wisdom rather than your own logical thinking and a BAII. As the sales process progresses, you reach a crucial moment where you sit with the financial advisor and your spouse at your kitchen table. With a sense of uncertainty, you ultimately utter those words that could have costly consequences, "I have complete trust in you." **I'll defer to your expertise and do whatever you believe is the best course of action."** You probably won't even spot the problem while you're accumulating money in the annuity but if you annuitize it (start taking the guaranteed payments for life) the problem surfaces but it's too late. Once you start receiving payments, you lose control of your principal. For example, my father contributed to an annuity for most of his life. He had paid thousands into this annuity over the years and when he was ready to start taking his money out, it was worth $70,000.

When my dad was ready to take money out of his annuity, he was given 4 options.

1. Take the $70,000 in a lump sum and pay the income Taxes on it. The trusted advisor refrained from informing my dad about the option to roll it into a self-directed IRA and defer the taxes.

2. Take what is called the income for life certain option and receive $4.29 for every $1,000 unit he had. Since he possessed $70,000 units, he would receive $300 per month for life.

3. Take a 10-life certain option that would pay him $3.95 per $1,000 per month ($3.95 X 70 = $276), guaranteeing that if he died, let's say in the 7th year, my mom would receive $276 per month for the next 3 years.

4. Choose the 20-year life certain option, which would cause a payment of $3 per $1,000 per month ($3.00 X 70 = $233). This option guarantees that if he were to pass away, let's say in the 7th year, my mom would receive $233 per month for the following 13 years.

With my mother's illness and my father's belief in his own longevity, he opted for the choice with the highest financial reward.

When he began receiving his guaranteed $300 per month for the rest of his life, he no longer had any rights to the lump sum principal of $70,000. My father died 3 months after receiving the first $300. My mother got a letter 2 weeks after he died starting the life annuity was over and the annuity company was going to keep the $70,000. The insurance company sent his $300 to him before his passing on the last day of the month. My mother cashed the check to help pay for the funeral. 30 days later, the insurance company sent her a demand letter demanding that she sends them back the $300. Do you really think that is what my father had in mind? While safety and guaranteed interest rates are good, you will want to put your money somewhere simple, watch the fees associated with these programs, and you will want to find a vehicle that will allow you to get your principal and interest back.

If I were aware of mortgage notes when this tragedy occurred, I could have rescued the situation for my mother. If my father would have rolled the $70,000 into a self-directed IRA. There would not be any taxes or penalties. It was possible for him to purchase these two notes in his IRA for $62,970. They would've compensated him with a monthly payment of $1,171. In other terms, she had the potential to withdraw an additional $871 per month, which is nearly four times the amount the annuity would provide. She possessed the choice to continue receiving $300 per month and deposit the additional $871 into the IRA, resulting in a remaining balance of $7,030 ($70,000 - $23,970 - $39,000 = $7,030). In under 11 months, she gained the capability to purchase another note for $16,000.

Which would pay $245 a month. So, she would then have $1,416 income even after my father died.

This is my personal experience with annuities, and you might be able to feel the anger seeping through my words. Here is an example of one of my clients' experiences with annuities. Annuities can offer a guaranteed income for life, but not a guaranteed return on investment (what I like to call your net effected yield). That's kind of a hard sentence to understand so here is an example of what a schoolteacher client of mine was sold. She was told that if she put $10,000 up front and $80 a month in this annuity for 20 years, they would pay her 5%. After talking to me she called the company and got a rundown of all the fees she was paying: 1.4% for administrative expenses, 1.1% for a rider to lock in the 5% annual return, 1.2% for a mortality expense fee, wrap fees, and an adviser fee, which together totaled 5.8%. These weren't all the fees; there was a surrender fee for the first 8 years, starting at 8% finally dropping to 0 after 8 years. I calculated what she was really making with her guaranteed 5%. In Wallet Money she was only making 4%. She asked me how can that be true, they guaranteed me 4%? I told her she was correct; they did guarantee they would pay 4% but they didn't guarantee how much of the $80 a month they were going to pay it on. They took their fees out before they paid the 4% return. They were charging her $20 in fees so she was only earning 2.3% because only $60 per month was going into the account. Instead of having $51,666 at the end of 20 years, she would only have $40,230. She surrendered her policy and paid the surrender charge. She was delighted that she discovered about the matter earlier instead of during her retirement. Don't postpone understanding your annuity until the last moment. Acquiring an annuity is similar to purchasing a time share. Once you realize that you've been screwed it's hard to get unscrewed.

As she received the distressing update about her guaranteed annuity's financial loss, her face flushed with anger. The sharp sound of the news pierced the silence, echoing in her ears. The scent of frustration filled the air, mingling with the tension that had suddenly engulfed the room. The weight of betrayal settled on her shoulders, causing her muscles to tense up as she contemplated the impending surrender charge. The sudden realization hit her like a punch in the gut. The sight of her bank statements, once a source of assurance, now mocked her. The sound of crumpling paper echoed her frustration as she clenched her fists in anger. The smell of ink and regret filled the room, intensifying her irritation. The weight of all those wasted years pressed heavily on her chest, leaving her seething with resentment. She calculated that she should have had about $16,000 but after paying all those fees and surrender charges she only had $12,000. All those fees and charges were written in the 170-page booklet the annuity company gave her so she would fully understand what she was buying. Both her and my dad clearly didn't understand what they were buying and simply trusted someone to advise them.

*****

Chapter 33

$20,000 Mortgage Notes

Again, at the time, I was unaware of mortgage notes, but if I possessed that knowledge, she could have utilized that $12,000 to purchase this note. It would've provided her with a monthly payment of $300. In only 13 months, she would have completely recovered all her surrender charges and fees.

Why Small Mortgage Notes Are Better Than Large Ones

Large Mortgage Notes

1. It takes a lot of money to buy one ($60,000 to $500,000)

2. The payments are high and hard to make when things go bad.

3. The payments are high and can be catastrophic to your cash flow if they are not paid.

4. There are large fluctuations in the property's value.

5. The insurance and taxes are high.

6. There are many more foreclosures in the upper range of homes.

7. People who have high house payments also have high debt and low reserves.

8. The odds of a high payment house, paying off early are smaller.

9. All your eggs are in one basket.

10. Unemployment isn't enough to make large payments.

Small Mortgage Notes or Real Estate Notes

1. You can buy 6 or 7 notes for $60,000.

2. The payments average $325 per month.

3. If you have 6 notes paying $325 per month the delay in one of them isn't catastrophic.

4. Very few fluctuations can be observed in moderately priced homes. A $70,000 is a $70,000 no matter if the real estate market is good or bad.

5. Insurance and taxes are low.

6. Few foreclosures occur in the moderate home range due to the average loan to value ratio

of 42% and monthly payments averaging $325. Where would anyone go to get a lower payment?

7. The odds of 1 of 6 notes paying off early are 6 times better than 1 large note paying off early.

8. It's better to diversify your investment.

9. Someone collecting $1,500 to $2,000 a month can still make their house payment.

The average homeowner either refinances or moves every 5 to 7 years. No numerical values are present on these small notes, and it is uncertain if they move earlier or later than the average.

If they pay the loan off you get the remaining balance on the original note.

If the owner pays the Birmingham house off in 1 year, you will get $16,697 plus the 12 payments of $250, which is $3,000 = $19,697 - the $14,500 you paid = $5,197 profit.

FV = -$19,697 How much you collected

N = 12 Months from the time you bought the note till paid off.

PV = $14,500 your investment.

PMT -$250 Payment you received each month.

CPT Yield = 49.91%

The worst case is they go term (120 months) then you make 15.77%.

If they pay it off in 12 months, you make 49.91%.

Following that, you can take the $19,697 and purchase another note. Remember, I mentioned one of the most crucial items to consider on my list is the amount per thousand invested per month. In this particular case, the amount was $17.24. So, if you purchased another note and it generated the same monthly amount, you would receive a payment of $339.57 instead of $250 without altering your coat.

The Difference Between Mortgage Notes and Discount Mortgage Notes

The difference between mortgage notes and discount mortgage notes is like the difference between submarines and sail boats. Mortgage notes are good for both the seller and the buyer however the buyer of a discount mortgage note makes a huge profit.

The first thing I will do to make this perfectly clear is to explain how mortgage notes work.

*****

Chapter 34

Real Estate, Gold, and Appreciation

The sight of gleaming skyscrapers and sprawling properties, and the glimmer of shimmering gold bars are often associated with the two best conventional wisdom investments. However, amidst the cacophony of bustling construction sites and the faint scent of freshly printed money, both real estate and gold reveal their major problems. Real estate needs to be rented out or sold to turn a profit. Gold offers safety but you can't take advantage of the most powerful force in the universe, compound interest. Most appreciation in real estate is currently inactive. I don't know about you but I don't like it when my money sleeps on the job. Let me explain what I mean by sleeping on the job. If you purchased a house valued at $100,000 and rented out the property, after 10 years, the value of the house had increased to $135,000. That $35,000 worth of equity would just remain unused. The time value of money tells my common sense that is surely a waste of resources. $35,000 divided by

10 Years is $290 per month. If you invested $290 per month into say a mortgage note that paid 14% in ten years you would have $76,445 but if it just sits in equity, you have $35,000 worth of equity. Wake your money up and put it to work.

*****

Chapter 35

Student Loans

I heard on the news yesterday that approximately $30,000 in student loans is held by 7 out of 10 college graduates. When we Baby Boomers graduated college, our parents might have had less money, but we didn't accumulate any debt. We got married, started a family, got a job, and bought a house. This time was called the Housing Boom. We possessed the income to purchase and sustain the American Dream, a house. Today, when college graduates get out of school, they need to get a job and start paying their student loan back. Marriages are happening later and later. Home purchases are almost impossible for young adults. This will influence the housing industry. Who will be the buyers of new homes? Millennials will probably never realize the American Dream and the Baby

Boomers will be completely out of the home buying market. Low end rental property will become a premium.

One other effect of this debt will be that young adults who are paying off student loans can't afford to save for their retirement. This alone will lower the amount of money going into the market and severely delay their savings for their retirement and when you add in their increased cost for health insurance, the death spiral steepens.

I know this sounds depressing, but if my Crystal Ball Common Sense Predictor is right, you have time to not only survive this perfect storm but to actually profit from it greatly. You wouldn't be reading this book if you hadn't already figured out that real estate was the commonsense answer to escaping the psycho stock market. So, let's see the bright side of the road. Here is how not only to take shelter from the storm but to prosper.

*****

Chapter 36

Fix, Flip, and Finance

The 4 Problems with fix and flip. Residual income.

My advice is to get in, get your money and get out. This is almost impossible to do, especially if you're just getting started. Newcomers and seasoned veterans are finding the plethora of governmental regulation obstructing their economic plans.

Dodd-Frank has succeeded in virtually choking the small mortgage out of existence. To protect the little guy, lawmakers have restricted the lender's ability to make money. By reducing the amount, a lender can charge on notes under $100,000 lenders and find small notes are not worth their time. The same amount of effort is required for a $50,000 loan as for a $500,000 loan, except the lender doesn't earn much profit on the smaller loan.

That makes me think of the story of the angler who was out on the lake fishing. He perceived a thump on the side of his boat and glanced over to see what it was. He was taken aback by the sight of a snake with a frog in its mouth. The angler had sympathy for the frog so he seized the snake and had it release the frog. The frog swam ashore, and the angler was filled with satisfaction about the good deed he had done, but then he looked at the sad snake in his hand and started experiencing remorse about the snake. He searched for something to feed the snake, but he did not come with any food. Yet, he arrived with a bottle of exquisite whiskey. Carefully, he poured a small amount into the snake's mouth before returning the snake to the water. The snake swam off quite content and the fisherman once again experienced a positive emotion until he heard another bump on the side of the boat. When he glanced over, he was once again taken aback to observe the snake's return, but this time it had 2 frogs in its mouth. You need to be careful of what you do, even if you have good intentions, because you get the behavior that you reward. Dodd Franks reward banks that make big loans and punishes banks that make small loans.

*****

Chapter 37

The 3 Fs

The new thing is called “The 3 Fs;” which stands for Fix, Flip, and Finance. In the old economy with liberal banking regulation, investors would simply fix and flip. The buyers encountered minimal difficulty in obtaining loans. It is impossible to say that today. Many opportunities exist to purchase, renovate, and sell properties. However, securing a loan qualification for someone can be as challenging as the back end of a shooting gallery. Many Fix and Flippers have been struggling against the "Banking Regulatory Wall" with minimal outcomes other than a wounded head. Implementing the new regulations has created an almost insurmountable obstacle for a small home buyer looking to purchase an affordable house. This complicates the process of flipping a fix and flip house. Time is money when you are a Fix and Flipper and waiting for someone to be approved for a loan can become expensive quickly.

After the recent economic downturn, millions of people now have such poor credit it is a chore to find a qualified buyer. A few people in the lower income bracket were able to avoid the recession with good credit.

Many experienced Fixes and Flip investors recently reached a consensus that the profit from the "flip" aspect of fix and flip has significantly dwindled. Bank underwriting guidelines severely restrict the amount that the Fix and Flipper can charge for the house. Banks have taken control of the flippers' ability to determine their own price. The Flipper is unable to sell a property for what the market will bear but must sell the property based on the value determined by an appraisal. Since the banks control the appraisals, the banks are in fact controlling the price flippers can charge. If your owner finances the property, you become the bank then you can find out for yourself what the true market value is.

The same thing goes for credit scores. Even though credit scores play a minor role in how individuals finance a home they own, they have substantially diminished the market's scope. I've said it before and will probably say again that when collateral was invented, the world started spinning faster. Protecting equity is inherent to human nature. If the Flipper owner finances the house, the Flipper becomes the bank so the Flipper can control the underwriting guidelines. Instead of using government mandated conventional wisdom guidelines the Flipper could use good old common sense and desire for profit.. One of the secrets of owner finance is the size of the down payment. The bigger the down payment, the more equity the owner has and the more collateral the note buyer receives. That increases the homeowner's fear of loss.

*****

Chapter 38

Down payment

I used to train car sales agents. The ones I have trained always made more money than the sales agents I didn't train simply because I taught them how to get bigger down payments. I realized that a larger down payment leads to greater profits. When selling a house with the owner's finance, you will have many buyers who can be encouraged to compete in bidding on down payments. Down payments make them have a fear of loss. Which makes the loan much better. The fear of loss will prompt the equity-rich homeowner to quickly pursue refinancing or selling the property.

Chapter 39

Owner Finance

I realized that the owner finance market is not growing as rapidly as the demand I observe. As more and more people realize how profitable mortgage notes are the prices will begin to climb and the discounts will begin to shrink. Plus, I recommend the smaller notes and I solved my problem; I found a way to create small notes. I was aware of the fact that a significant number of individuals had $20,000 in their 401ks and IRAs compared to those with $100,000. So, if you are the person I'm referring to, you will find this interesting. I knew there were many people who wanted to do income property. To do income property, you must have some money. Getting a loan on income property isn't easy. So those people have a hard time financing low end income property. In my opinion, low end income property is the next boom.

Remember the perfect storm, well let's apply some of those facts. The Baby Boomers loved to the American Dream, they wanted to own a home. When they turned 55 or so, they were up to their ears in credit card debt and many of them went to their friendly bank and refinanced their mortgage at a lower rate. They had confidence in their ability to borrow their way out of debt. Once I saw a Simpson TV show where Homer was digging a hole. He dug so deep he couldn't get out so he decided to just dig up. They were able to reduce their payments, but giving up all their equity was required. The problem was they didn't change their spending habits and within a few years they were deep in debt again.

Ten years later, the perfect storm hits and upper end real estate takes a hit. The house lost some of its value. Now they are up-side-down. They are ready to retire. Let's say their house payment is $1,500. When they retire they start pulling $3,000 out of their 401k; them and thousands of other Baby Boomers who are in the same fix. At age 70 1/2 even if they didn't retire they will be forced to start withdrawing. As more and more Baby Boomers start to withdraw the mutual fund manager must sell shares to pay them their $3,000. I will take 20 young people putting $150 in their 401k to equal one Baby Boomer, pulling out $3,000. Because the price of the shares will shoot down the manager will be forced to sell more shares, which will speed up the downward direction of the stock market. Just because the numbers on the stock market may still be high, you're not considering the impact of inflation, which creates the illusion of the stock market going up. Soon the Baby Boomer will run out of money and when that happens he won’t be able to make his $1,500 a month payment. The first thing he will try to do is sell the house but like I said he’s up-side-down. He owes more than it’s worth. To recap his position, he’s out of money, he’s retired so he has no income, he can’t sell his house because he owes more than it’s worth. He can’t get financed in a smaller home for all the reasons I listed above. But he does now qualify for Section 8 rental assistance. The government will help with the rent. That is one of the reasons I mentioned earlier that "Low End Rental Property" is on the verge of becoming the next big thing.

There will need to be a lot of low-end rental properties to fill the market demand. Luckily, there are already many people who want to do “Fix and Flip” and rental property. These people will be your source for discount mortgage notes. There is no industry attempting to finance low-end rental property and none exploiting Section 8. To qualify for Section 8 to provides financial assistance for decent, safe, and sanitary housing to eligible households whose annual gross income does not exceed 50% of HUD's median income guidelines. HUD requires 75% of all new households admitted to the program to be at or below 30% of the area median income.

What that means is if you rent to someone who qualifies the government will either pay the rent or supplement it. That's a guaranteed payment to the owner. This is normally used for apartments but can be used for rental property. In fact, Section 8 will help the renters become owners.

What you want to do is locate a Fix and Flipper, I like them more than people who want to own a house from now on. I would run an ad on Craigs List that read like this. **"We finance Fix and Flippers on low-income rentals. Up to $20,000. No credit check or Social Security number needed."** You can imagine the number of calls I would get. I didn't care where the property was located. In fact, I did a lot of business in Detroit. I don't mind the location since I would never have to handle repairs or concern myself with rent collection. I was simply the first position lien holder, (I was the bank). When someone called on my ad I would have them video a "walk through" of the house and then I would pull comps. I would only lend up to $20,000. But I would also help them locate a Section 8 renter. I made connections with some women shelters in the area and they would refer women who already qualified for Section 8. Currently, a waiting list ranging from 4 to 6 months exists, indicating high demand.

Since the purpose of the whole thing was to Fix and Flip, Section 8 made it easy to flip the property. I would attend real estate investment clubs and at the end of the meeting, I would let the members know that there was a 3-bedroom house available for rent at $1,000 with a Section 8 tenant living in it. It was possible for them to purchase it for $40,000.

Let me explain why after lending the Fix and Flipper I would help him or her sell it. The mortgage note the Fix and Flipper signed was structured like this; It was a 3 year note at 15% interest only. After the first year, with payments of $250 it converted to a 2-year fully amortized loan and the payments jumped to $693. No matter when the house was flipped in the first year the borrower must pay the entire year's payment or $3,000 minus any payments he or she already paid. So, let's say they flipped the house after two months for $40,000. They would pay you $20,000 and $2,500 for the rest of the first-year payments. They made $17,500 in two months. If they did three more that year they would make $70,000. Plus, they were collecting $1,000 per month and only paying you $250. This is a win, win, win. How many of these deals do you think they want to do a year? You would just keep lending them money and they will keep doing Fix and Flip.

If they don't sell the house the first year then the payments go up to $693 and they are still cash flowing $307 a month. At the end of the third year, they own the house free and clear. So, people told me I would find no one who would pay me 15%. My reply was to ask a question. "How much money did the Fix and Flipper have invested?" "Zero" "Now that's a huge return on a Zero investment."

How much did I make on a deal like this? If they sold the house in two months, then I got my $20,000 back plus $2,500 interest. I made 72.79%, interest on my guaranteed loan. The faster they sell the house the higher my return. That's why I helped them rent and sell the house. I said this was a win, win, win scenario; The renter gets a refurbished house that the government subsidizes the rent. The Fix and Flipper makes $17,500 on a zero investment and the lender made 72.79% on their investment.

*****

Chapter 40

How to Find the Money to do Notes

In 1913, almost all the congressional representatives were wealthy businessmen. At the time the only income the federal government collected was from tariffs, duties and fees that were paid by the businesses. The wealthy business-owning congressional representative decided that they would rather the average wage earner pay for the federal government instead of them, so they told the average wage earner that we needed an income tax.

They informed us it would indeed be a tax on the rich because (we must have been extremely naïve back then. The average wage earner was the parent of many children and could claim them as dependents, and due to their charitable nature, they could deduct charitable donations. The banks possessed a significant amount of money that they desired to lend to the average citizen, allowing us to deduct the interest we paid them. This might have been the start of our current debt society because no matter what interest rate they charged you could simply write the interest off your income taxes. The business owners diligently recorded their expenses, discovering that nearly every item could be written off yet the average family couldn't take advantage of this tax break because they didn't own a business. We bought their story and passed a constitutional amendment to start an income tax. What were we thinking?

At the end of each year, we were supposed to send in whatever tax we owed, but the system didn't appear to work all that effectively. During World War II, amidst the urgent need for funds to fuel the war effort, a group of cunning masterminds devised a diabolical plan. They recognized that the Internal Revenue Service (IRS) had the potential to accumulate more resources by collecting income tax prior to the workers receiving their hard-earned wages. The sight of officials meticulously calculating, the sound of pens swiftly scribbling on paper, and the distinct scent of ink permeated the atmosphere. A sense of both urgency and discomfort remained as the government tirelessly chased after funds. Boy, were they right; revenues went up 1000%. Since most of the men were off to war and became accustomed to not making much money and having the government do everything for them, when they got back they just accepted that the tax was withheld before they got their check.

The average American overpays income taxes, resulting in something called a 'tax refund' by over $3,200 a year. We overpaid our taxes to the tune of $512 billion ($512,000,000,000). The IRS doesn't pay you interest on this money, they're borrowing it from you for free.

The IRS made the instructions for figuring the correct amount to withhold so complicated and the threat of an IRS audit so scary that the average American overpays income taxes resulting in something called a 'tax refund' by an average today of over $3,200 a year. The IRS doesn't even pay any interest on your voluntary overpayment.

Places to find the money you already have but don't know it.

The first money to go after is the easiest; tax refund: http://www.irs.gov/pub/irs-pdf/p15.pdf

The first money to go after is the easiest; tax refund:
www.irs.gov/ScheduleC and download a Schedule C.

Using the IRS's own instructions if you make $1,600 every 2 weeks and you got a $3,200 tax refund you are overpaying your taxes. A $3,200 refund ÷ 26 pay periods = $123 per pay period or $266.67 per month. If you examine your pay stub and notice that they are withholding $163 per check and now you realize you are paying $123 in excess, then subtract $123 from $163 to get $40. Direct your gaze towards the chart and observe how near you can come to $40. Change the withholding allowances to 6.

MARRIED Persons—**BIWEEKLY** Payroll Period

(For Wages Paid through December 2011)

And the wages are–		And the number of withholding allowances claimed is—										
At least	But less than	0	1	2	3	4	5	6	7	8	9	10
		The amount of income tax to be withheld is—										
$1,500	$1,520	$148	$127	$106	$84	$64	$49	$35	$21	$7	$0	$0
1,520	1,540	151	130	109	87	66	51	37	23	9	0	0
1,540	1,560	154	133	112	90	69	53	39	25	11	0	0
1,560	1,580	157	136	115	93	72	55	41	27	13	0	0
1,580	1,600	160	139	118	96	75	57	43	29	15	1	0
1,600	1,620	163	142	121	99	78	59	45	31	17	3	0

1. Divide the amount of your last refund by the number of paydays you get a year; If you get paid on the 1st and 15th then you're paid 26 times a year.
2. You just added 26 X $123= $3,198 to your paycheck or $266.50 per month.

Now add that $266.50 to your smallest monthly bill and pay it off quickly. Then use the freed-up amount to pay the next one. You will see very quickly you get out of debt and free up that money to use to invest.

*****

Chapter 41

Just Do the Math

Let me show you the math. Understanding this becomes easier with the possession of a $30 Texas Instruments BA II Plus calculator. Let's assume the note you are looking at was originally $100,000, at 0% for 30 years, with payments of $277.78 per month. The borrower has made 120 payments, and the payoff is $66,666. With 20 years to go. You may wonder, how can I make money on a zero present loan? Well, here's the math. In your BA II, you would enter 240 on the 2nd (Number of remaining months). Enter 13 in I/Y (interest rate). The resulting amount will equal $23,709. You should buy this note for $23,709 to make 13%.

If you don't currently possess a BA II, simply trust me and when you are able to acquire the program for your phone, it will significantly impact your life.

The advantage for you becomes clear when you are comparing one note against another to see how hard your money is working for you.

In specific areas, that you have cash is overlooked.

1. If you're 62 or older and own equity in your home you should check on doing a reverse mortgage. Reverse mortgages are a HUD program enabling you to access your equity while you are alive. You will not be required to make any payments as long as you or your spouse are alive, even though you still possess your house. If both of you die the house goes to your heirs. They are given a time frame of 6 months to either sell the property or refinance it. The Boggy Man does not exist. They will lend you about 50 to 60% of its value. This is an example. I don't sell reverse mortgages so you will need to check with someone that does. If you're 62 and your house is now worth $200,000 and you still owe $50,000 with payments of $1,000 a month, they will lend you about $100,000. You use $60,000 from the amount to pay off your mortgage. This implies you have no obligation for a house payment. It is necessary for you to keep paying the insurance and taxes. You not only accumulate savings of $1,000 per month

but also possess a tax-free cash amount of $40,000.

2. If you have a cash value life insurance policy pull out your cash value. You still have ownership of your policy and you are not required to repay the insurance. The face amount is reduced by your withdrawal.
3. Borrow money from your 401k. You will repay the amount, but the payments will be made to yourself. Penalties or taxes do not exist.
4. Partner up with someone. You supply the knowledge and they supply the money. Once a deal is completed, the funding will sustain itself.

I accomplished this with no funds and this is the method I employed. I put an ad on Craige's List that read; "We finance Fix and Flipper up to $20,000. No credit checks or SS# needed."

That ad connected me with Fix and Flippers whom I was able to explain my system to. After hearing the details of the loan, they all wanted to do it. Then I put an ad on Craige's List that read; "If you want to get 401k or IRA out of this crazy market and get a guaranteed 15% interest that is backed by collateral. Call this number 555-555-5555.

I've already explained how both of these things work but let me explain what I tell the leader.

If you lend this Fix and Flipper $20,000 at 15% (interest only) for 36 months with payments of $250 per month. You get the first lien on the property. If the Flipper sales the house in the first year you get $3,000. If he sales in the first month you get your $20,000 back plus $3,000 that's 195% percent return. If the Flipper doesn't sell it in the first year the note converts to a two-year fully amortized loan. You made 15% interest the first year. The flipper now pays $969 per month. After those two years the house is paid off. You collected 24 X $969= $23,273 plus the $3,000 the first year, that's $26,273 in three years fully guaranteed.

If he agrees to lend the money I tell him I don't have a borrower right now but when I find one and I'll send him all the information and he can decide.

The Fix and Flipper would only receive $18,000 and I charged him $2,000 when the loan is made. The Flipper is not out a penny. You have the ability to do the same thing I did until you have enough money to lend the money yourself.

I understand that reading this book is like drinking from a fire hose and that it only increases your curiosity, but if you have any inquiries, I will be happy to talk with you. Call 737-293-6940 and leave me a message and I will call you back. If I can help I will.

*****

www.ingramcontent.com/pod-product-compliance
Lightning Source LLC
LaVergne TN
LVHW050821061126
851857LV00012B/911